DATE DUE

José Lezama Lima, Poet of the Image

University of Florida Monographs
Humanities Number 64

José Lezama Lima, Poet of the Image

Emilio Bejel

Illustrations by Vicente Dopico

University of Florida Press
Gainesville

The University of Florida Press is a member of University Presses of Florida, the scholarly publishing agency of the State University System of Florida. Books are selected for publication by faculty editorial committees at each of Florida's nine public universities: Florida A&M University (Tallahassee), Florida Atlantic University (Boca Raton), Florida International University (Miami), Florida State University (Tallahassee), University of Central Florida (Orlando), University of Florida (Gainesville), University of North Florida (Jacksonville), University of South Florida (Tampa), University of West Florida (Pensacola).

Orders for books published by all member presses should be addressed to University Presses of Florida, 15 NW 15th Street, Gainesville, FL 32603.

Contents

Acknowledgments

As I think back over the past decade and the people who consistently offered advice and encouragement on the study of Lezama's work, I immediately recall Ramiro Fernández, Rubén Ríos-Ávila, Roberto González Echevarría, Justo Ulloa, and Leonor Álvarez de Ulloa.

It has become a routine to preface all my works with mention of Ramiro, yet, in all honesty, it could be no other way. We began to seriously study Lezama together in 1973, and since then have held endless conversations about the man and his work.

By 1978 I had drafted my first essay on Lezama, "*Muerte de Narciso*: hacia la indiferenciación o el Paraíso" (I would publish it years later), and Roberto González Echevarría introduced me to Rubén Ríos-Ávila, who, while at Cornell and under the direction of Roberto, was writing his doctoral thesis on Lezama. As part of his research, Rubén had read my essay in manuscript. Ever since, Rubén, Roberto, and I have often discussed the various aspects of Lezama's work. I have relied on Rubén's brilliant comparison of Lezama and Mallarmé, and I have been enlightened by Roberto's study of the relationship between Góngora and Lezama.

Two other friends who have helped in much the same way are Justo Ulloa and Leonor Álvarez de Ulloa; both are dedicated to the study of Lezama. Justo's doctoral thesis (1973) on Lezama and Sarduy was the first extensive study I encountered that dealt with what was to become the central issue of the present text. Both Justo and Leonor are noted *lezamistas*, recognized for essays, lectures, and invaluable bibliographical work.

During the mid-seventies, I met Enrico Mario Santí, who was soon to join the growing group of Lezama scholars in the United

States. Today his articles on Lezama's *Paradiso* and *Oppiano Licario* are indispensable. I want to mention here Efraín Barradas, who in 1978 wrote a Princeton dissertation on *Orígenes*, and has since published important articles on Lezama. It was through Efraín's studies that I was led to investigate the literary context in which Lezama developed his early work. I thank Daniel Balderston and Ester Gimbernat de González for their support of the present book. Daniel gave me very good advice on style. Ester's book on *Paradiso* is an important contribution to a better understanding of Lezama's major novel.

Another friend and very important Lezama scholar whose insightful works on Lezama I have read with great interest is Julio Ortega. During the past few years I have been in contact with Gustavo Pellón, who has published interesting works on Lezama's writings and political context. And then there is Pedro Lastra. I cannot recall how often Pedro took the time to discuss with me Lezama's focus and style.

For assistance received during my visits to Cuba since 1978, I thank Ambrosio Fornet, Cintio Vitier, Fina García Marruz, Miguel Barnet, Reynaldo González, Nancy Morejón, Manuel Moreno Fraginals, César López, José Prats Sariol, José Rodríguez Feo, Antón Arrufat, and Abel Prieto. And though this list of names is long (and I am probably forgetting someone), all of them, in some way or another, helped bring about the present volume.

I thank Lori Madden, Ron Koss, and Larry Lyall for dedicating many hours to the revision and editing of this text during the final stages of preparation. Lori, one of my doctoral students at the University of Florida, has a thorough knowledge of English and Spanish and a discerning intelligence. Ron and I dedicated several weeks to the stylistic refinement of this text, and I benefited greatly from his intense and methodical editorial expertise in preparing the final draft. I also relied on Larry's considerable stylistic and editorial skills; his knowledge not only of English and Spanish but also of literature and the humanities in general often offered a refreshing perspective.

Finally, there is the ongoing support I enjoy from my colleagues at the University of Florida. I want to mention in particular Raymond Gay-Crosier, who, in his capacity as department chairperson, encouraged me in the completion of this book and also gave me a full semester (Fall 1987) away from my classes so that I might have the time to concentrate on the final stages of revision. I am also grateful to my fellow Spanish Americanists Reynaldo Jiménez, Andrés Avellaneda, and Adolfo Prieto, who have helped in so many ways over the past five years.

Introduction

Most critics of Spanish American literature agree that José Lezama Lima (Cuba, 1910–76) is one of the truly universal writers of our time. His style, his poetic vision, and the unique role he defines for literature have been a continuing influence in Cuba, as well as throughout Latin America. However, it is only fairly recently that his work and its critical interpretations have begun to appear in languages other than Spanish.

Lezama's monumental production includes several volumes of poetry, collections of essays, two novels, and a few short stories, yet each piece is part of an ambitious literary project that articulates what Lezama calls his "Poetic System of the World." Among those Spanish American contemporaries who dealt in thoroughgoing cosmologies, Lezama can only be compared with Jorge Luis Borges; and among those whose strengths lie in imaginative creativity, his work compares favorably to that of Gabriel García Márquez.

Lezama intended his project as a contribution to what he called "the great symbolist current, which flows from the powerful Dante to the delightful Mallarmé."[1] Moreover, *Paradiso*, his most important novel, has prompted several critics to suggest its similarity to Proustian narrative. My own observations have led me to compare the poetry of Lezama and that of Wallace Stevens, a frequent contributor to Lezama's magazine, *Orígenes*.

This book takes into account most of Lezama's literary work. Aside from the detailed explication, analysis, and interpretation of the texts, it situates Lezama's poetic vision in relation to several significant artistic and philosophical currents. Attention is given to the relationship between the work of Lezama and that of Alejo Carpentier, Sor Juana Inés de la Cruz, and other Spanish American writers, as well as to Lezama's work in relation to that of Dante, Vico, Hegel, Nietzsche, Heidegger, Spengler, Mallarmé, and Valéry.

I give special consideration to Lezama's articulation of the complex interplay between subject, writing, nature, and history. The thread that runs throughout the book is Lezama's vision of the Image as the creative power stemming from a fundamental lack of natural order. In the first chapter I focus on Lezama's sense of *Image* and *subject* as contrasted with the "representative writing" of literary realism, the neoclassical definition of "Nature," and the romantic idea of "subject." The second chapter explores the relationship between the Lezamian subject and poetic discourse and establishes the critical perspective from which I develop a detailed study of his two most important narrations, *Paradiso* and *Oppiano Licario*, the concerns of chapters 3 and 4, respectively. In these chapters I elaborate the idea of a subject in crisis caught up in the conflict between his or her separation from the world and from language. Here I show how this "subject in crisis" seeks to resolve this conflict by way of the poetic strategies that comprise Lezama's poetic vision. Finally, in chapter 5, I discuss the Lezamian historical perspective as a contribution to authentic Latin American expression, within which the Latin American "subject" weaves a metaphorical history, a poetical history, out of the circumstance of marginality. This perspective emphasizes the "absence" that provokes a powerful creativity.

Lezama assures us that "only the difficult is stimulating,"[2] and his work is truly one of the most complex and difficult ever written in Spanish. The reader must take an entirely different path from the accustomed response to representative art. Lezama is opposed to any art that is "readily understood," that "clearly" mirrors a self-sufficient world that language presumes to articulate with accuracy. For Lezama, the world is not a preestablished entity that language, in a passive role, can faithfully represent. To the contrary, Lezama's poetry is a means of knowledge per se, which metaphorically penetrates the world in order to give meaning to what is without meaning. His poetic quest embraces the exceptional and the excessive as strategies by which he pointedly challenges established limits, strategies that aim toward a visionary answer, which will, paradoxically, negate any possibility of totality.

His passionate concern with the interplay among subject, writing, nature, and history prompts us to examine his texts and question our own methods of interpretation and analysis. In this book I deliberately avoid the methodology of structuralism that occupied me during the 1970s.[3] Instead, I adopt a critical approach that does not depend on any specific critical school. This approach has evolved from my reflections on various contemporary critical currents as well as my reading of the "literary" texts themselves.

For the most part, I assume that a critic's function is to be occupied with the analysis and interpretation of the work at hand and not with a "search for the author behind the text." This emphasis can be related to the Saussurian attempt to de-authorize language, but it is an idea also found in much contemporary criticism. Moreover, in this book I do not use Lezama's texts as a pretext for validating a preestablished critical system. My reading of Lezama's texts has prompted me to reflect on not only what they teach me but also what it is about them that I enjoy.

The richness of Lezama's work cannot but astonish us as well as induce us to admit the impossibility of exhaustive explication. However, this difficulty can also be an invitation to engage Lezama on his own terms and risk a dynamic, if nondefinitive, interpretation of his work. I have often taken recourse in Lezama's observation that it is what we do not understand that marks the historical and progressive penetration into the difficult. To this we might add that, were it not for the difficult and the mysterious, there would be little of what we call history. Furthermore, we would lack the incentive necessary to continue the critical process. The following interpretations are drawn from a multiplicity of options that each text offers. Those I have chosen to emphasize seem to me to follow a definite pattern of textual development. I have come to believe that three central factors contribute to the interpretation of any text: the elements of the text itself, the particular historical epoch in which the text is read, and the subjective and ideological characteristics of the reader.

Regarding my approach here, I sometimes resort to an "internal" study of the texts themselves, a textual analysis that relies on Lezama's poetics. At other times I focus on the "external," comparing, interpreting, and placing Lezama's work in relation to other artistic and philosophical currents. The latter perspective also takes in the possible symbolic relationships between the texts and their social context. This dual approach (the "internal" and the "external") allows me to consider not only "what is written" but also "about what it is written," about what the text has concerned itself with. But when I deal with the historical context, I do not intend to imply that this enables us to grasp "the truth" or "the concrete." I believe that when we express in language a historical event, we remove that event to a symbolic plane and can only make reference to the "historical" from this symbolic perspective. Past events are never faithfully reproduced in discourse. Perhaps by reminding ourselves that critical discourse also falls within this symbolic plane and must express itself in a metaphorical language, we can better emphasize the ongoing awareness of not only "what is written" and "about what it is written" but also "how the text is read."

When an ambitious view such as Lezama's radically questions an entire constellation of prevailing concepts, attitudes, ideas, and historical periods, it can result in nothing less than a profound change in the manner in which we regard this heritage. Furthermore, a careful reading of Lezama's texts, which demand a different kind of reading, opens new avenues between ideas, works, and historical periods. Thus the question of where to situate Lezama's work in the "history of culture" demands a rather complex answer, which must take into account a specific manner of reading that "history of culture."

This very book is, in one sense, an attempt to read anew. However, in this introduction I will limit myself to a brief sketch of *one* of the possible interpretations of Lezama's work: the fundamentally Orphic nature of his poetic vision. I adopt this approach because I believe that a familiar metaphor is the best vehicle for introducing my study of Lezama.

For Lezama, the Image is an obscure, creative force; hence all creativity originates in the mysterious. This origin is similar to the Hades into which Orpheus descended before returning with only a flower as proof that he had visited the source of creativity. In his role as Orphic poet, Lezama assimilates many metaphors from the occultist tradition. Among other things, Lezama's fascination with the Orphic explains his interest in Taoism, *tokonoma*, and his concern with Neoplatonism. The Tao is similar in many ways to the Lezamian Image. It is an expression of successive mutations that evolve from nonbeing to being, from absence to image. In the same sense, the *tokonoma* is an absence that creates from within a vacuum. And, of course, the Neoplatonic concept of a world of potential form as the generative force for the created world is part of the Orphic tradition. Lezama's Orphism is a metaphor taken from a variety of cultures yet founded in an unorthodox assimilation of Catholicism. In Catholic mythology, Christ, like Orpheus, descended into Hell and returned to this world with the poetic possibility of Resurrection.

Lezama's Orphic elaboration, which bases itself upon a generative Image, reminds one of Dante's theory of the image, especially as found in *Paradiso* (clearly a model for Lezama's most important novel). Dante's belief that "high fantasy" is the most sublime function of the imagination is wonderfully represented by the Dantescan poet who entertains visions of an earthly Paradise without the aid of Virgil, the symbol of human reason. One of Dante's most enduring contributions assimilated by Lezama was the elevation of the poetic imagination over conceptual reason.

Lezama's Orphism derives its historical perspective from Catholicism, more specifically the Augustinian concept of *logos spermaticos*. Augustine proposes that history unfolds from a creative power that, in its original state, was seamless potential. This suggests an interplay among an irreversible unfolding and a static archetype, which serves as both anchor and source for creative energy. From this, Lezama elaborates the idea of "imaginary eras" as part of the historical process, which is actually the Image realizing itself in Time. This idea is similar to Vico's: history as the realization of Providence manifesting itself in a series of epochs.

Lezama also responded to Vico's articulation of "poetic wisdom," the process by which knowledge is obtained via the image and not through conceptual reason. In fact, Lezama believed that Vico's perspective was a direct answer to Cartesian rationalism and was part of a marginal tradition that opposes rational metaphysics in Western thought. Lezama thought that the development of this tradition was a "symbolist current" that ran from Dante to Mallarmé and included Vico. Vico had begun to note the fragmentation in modern rationalism, which he characterized as a fault in modern culture. Lezama, like Vico, valued not only image over concept but also the mythic over the factual. Thus his vision goes beyond both Cartesian rationalism and English empiricism, since it is the Image that is the basic force for the acquisition of knowledge.

Lezama's work invites us to reconsider the tenets of contemporary culture (or at least a few of its interpretations). Lezama does not intend a total negation of Christian values. To the contrary, he encourages critical assimilation of many of these values. This distinguishes his perspective from Nietzsche's, especially in regard to Christianity and classical antiquity. Lezama interprets Nietzsche as criticizing the lack of creativity in Greek culture, which, for Lezama, contains a powerful creative force represented by the mythical figure of Dionysus. Lezama insists with equal emphasis that Nietzsche's greatest error was his attempt to subvert all Christian values, since Nietzsche's subversion would do away with what Lezama considered to be essential for both Christianity and the Hellenic view (Orphism and Pythagorianism in particular). In Lezama's opinion, Nietzsche's negation of Greek and medieval culture led him to overemphasize Renaissance values, an emphasis that Lezama questioned. Instead of negating the values of classical antiquity and Christianity, Lezama proposes their critical assimilation. From this standpoint, he challenges the many cultural theorists who argue that the only positive elements in contemporary culture began in the Renaissance. Furthermore, Lezama proposes the "symbolist current" as an integral part of contemporary culture and encourages the assimilation of Orphic and occult traditions.

Nevertheless, Lezama maintains a dialogue with Nietzsche that is far from negative. For example, he refers to the author of *Zarathustra* as "one of the most brilliant European thinkers in the past hundred years" and as one of the most incisive representatives of the "crisis of capitalist individualism in the nineteenth century."[4] Both authors arrive at a definition of the person as a creative subject involved in the process of self-realization. But Lezama emphasizes this insight through his vision of history as metaphorical construction. The meaning of history thus becomes a narrative process embracing equally the mythic and the historical. The idea of a "fictionalized history" echoes Nietzsche, though Lezama makes an important distinction when he emphasizes history as a positive progression. Here Lezama is closer to Nietzsche than to scientific methodology. And, ironically, Nietzsche is closer to medieval thought than to Renaissance thought.

It is important here to recall Heidegger's distinction between the methodology of scientific positivism and the intellectual process of the "essential thinker," by which he means Nietzsche.[5] This characterization might just as easily refer to Lezama. The scientist, though recognizing the limits of knowledge, never considers that the unknown cannot be known. The unknown is simply what we as yet do not know. To the contrary, the "essential thinker" accepts that there is an unknown region that can never be known, either rationally or scientifically. If the scientist asks in order to obtain utilitarian answers, the thinker asks to find the basis from which he or she can presume to ask the question. Yet for Lezama, to question at this profound level is to have already given an answer.

Lezama's interest in Nietzsche, Heidegger, Mallarmé, Joyce, Proust, and other writers who share his poetic orientation is based on the idea that these writers, within their distinct epochs and perspectives, signal important manifestations of a radical subversion of rationalist metaphysics. This subversion undermines the ideology grounded in rationalist abstraction, realistic representation, and subjective individualism. Lezamian cosmology can be defined as belonging to what some contemporary theorists call "postmodernism."[6] Specifically, it is a cosmology that chooses to begin its visionary process from the margins of rational metaphysics and privileges metaphorical discourse over the supposed objectivity of science and logic.

For Lezama, there is no final conceptual truth that serves as the goal for a philosophical quest. His discourse is incapable of stating totality since it is based in the unknown and its only medium is metaphor. But Lezama insists that this Orphic vision—founded in the unknown—does not imply desperation but rather a profound sense of happiness. In place of Heidegger's being-for-death, he proposes the metaphorical subject as being-for-resurrection.

There is no doubt that the Orphic quest for the mysterious and the unknown is a fundamental shared by Lezama and Mallarmé. Lezama praises the author of *Crise de Vers*, saying that his work "will one day be lifted up to be read by the gods."[7] But whereas the Mallarmean sense of absence leads to an absolute negation and frustration on the part of the subject-creator, Lezama's Image embraces both the subject and his language in a joyous celebration. For Lezama, absence is the force that draws all that is not yet created into a constant state of creation. He proposes a special sort of teleological unfolding toward a redeemable goal. Lezama's Image is not only *difference,* or *absence,* but also the source of a positive creativity.

The finest articulation of Lezama's poetics is his novel *Paradiso.* Here his poetic project is the weaving of a fictional subject whose threads are drawn from Lezama's personal life. The process is similar to Joyce's *Portrait of an Artist* or Proust's *Remembrance of Times Past*. Lezama develops the notion of Carlyle and Nietzsche that literary self-representation is an instance of self-fiction. Rather than re-presenting the subject as an object from the past, Lezama creates an "Other" who has been conceived by the imagination. This strategy is designed to confront the disjunction between identity and discourse. Lezama's Image strives to bring this discord into a metaphorical harmony between identity and discourse, between the subject and its self-representation. The process involves not only the relationship between subject, language, and nature but also Lezama's idea of history.

For Lezama, the Image always opens onto the future. History functions like a narrative process, a kind of *dramatis personae* shaped by the bits and pieces of a fragmented reality. The basis of Lezama's epic vision is his recognition that the romantic quest for complete self-realization is impossible yet absolutely necessary. Such a search is the invitation of the Image and can never be abandoned. This quest often appears dramatically during times of crisis as a response to a loss of orientation.

Lezama's history is thus a progressive unfolding whose continuity is guaranteed by a rebellious metaphorical subject. Regarding Latin America, Lezama propounds that this "subject" appeared in the eighteenth century as a result of the cultural symbiosis between indigenous cultures and the "decadence" of the European metropolis. Lezama also assimilates elements of those Americanists who have integrated the colonial past, reevaluated the Indian world, and brought about national and regional affirmation of Latin America. This perspective contrasts with the nineteenth-century liberal viewpoint that negates and despises the black, Indian, gaucho, and peasant cultures. Lezama distances himself from traditional liberal interpretations and integrates the contribution of the Cuban Revolution of 1959 to his theory of "imaginary eras." In this way, Lezama's vision of history is more radical than that propounded by both traditional liberal theorists and traditional Americanists. Lezama's subject is drawn from all social levels, ethnic and racial groups; in short, from all those who have stood in the way of a dominant cultural view opposed to cultural liberation. Lezama's vision of history adopts poetic strategies as a way to resolve at the symbolic level the tensions of historical context. Lezama always implies a movement toward a redeemable nature and a morally superior society.

Lezama Lima believed everything began with poetry. In one sense his cosmology is a reaction to the profound crisis in which he matured, a time best defined as "prosaic" in all senses of the term. Lezama was scarcely twenty when he took part in the student demonstration of 30 September 1930 against the dictatorship of Gerardo Machado (1925–33). The two decades preceding the poet's involvement with Cuba's revolutionary history were times of worldwide instability, and we can easily identify the tenor of a poet shaped by an era that had created an exile for artists within their own society. Lezama's poetics addresses the alienation of the 1930s, including the revolution against Machado, the interventionist policy of the United States, the Spanish Civil War, and the depression. Latin America saw the European crisis as a series of fragmentations that confirmed the dehumanization and decadence of Western civilization. Lezama reacted by creating a poetic universe, a counterpoint to these momentous circumstances.

Among the roads open to a young poet lies the possibility of retreating from the immediate in order to explore options and engage the contradictions of a demanding reality. In art, this "distancing" is often voiced as a utopian image, a symbolic substitute for the absence of hope. Lezama chose to write for an elite able to grasp his labyrinthian strategies. Although his response is optimistic in the midst of very negative circumstances, he is always aware of immediate reality. Thus his answer includes both his "alienation" and his hope for a morally renovated "new man." This is the stimulus for Lezama's later concern with the specifically "Latin American expression."

In an essay in the late 1960s, Lezama recalls his early years: "It was said the Cuban should be disabused, was disillusioned, insistently pessimistic, and had lost the true meaning of his symbols."[*8] Lezama is referring to his coming of age during the aborted revolution against Machado and his suffering under the Batista dictatorship (1952–58). He is the "Cuban" of the generation that included the young intellectuals who founded *Orígenes*, a magazine Lezama directed from 1944 until 1956. And though

---

* "Se decía que el cubano era un ser *desabusé*, que estaba desilusionado, que era un ensimismado pesimista, que había perdido el sentido profundo de sus símbolos."

these intellectuals have been called escapists, they were actually responsible for a hopeful cultural resistance.[9]

Through *Orígenes*, Lezama began to establish an international reputation. The magazine provided a forum for a group of authors that included Lezama and several of his contemporaries, as well as significant writers from throughout the world. He would often publish commentaries on the German translations that appeared in Ortega y Gasset's magazine, *Revista de occidente*. The context provided by *Orígenes* encouraged a new reading of Hegel and Spengler, among others. The French were represented by Rimbaud, Mallarmé, Valéry, Claudel, and Camus; and the surrealist school by Eluard and Aragon. Saint-John Perse was a particular favorite of Lezama's. English writers who often contributed were G. K. Chesterton, Virginia Woolf, Dylan Thomas, and, especially, T. S. Eliot, who was in frequent contact with the magazine's co-editor José Rodríguez Feo. The United States was well represented by George Santayana, William Carlos Williams, and Wallace Stevens.

Octavio Paz noted that *Orígenes* was one of the most important literary publications in Latin America. His mentor, Alfonso Reyes, was frequently included, as was Paz himself. Several of the now influential writers from the Spanish-speaking world were either contributors or the object of critical studies: Borges and Macedonio Fernández from Argentina; Vicente Aleixandre, Juan Ramón Jiménez, Vicente Gaos, Francisco Ayala, and María Zambrano from Spain (this last made a noteworthy impact on the editors); and from Cuba, Cintio Vitier, Fina García Marruz, Octavio Smith, Ángel Gaztelu, Gastón Baquero, Lorenzo García Vega, and Eliseo Diego, among the most notable.[10]

Lezama's generation lived amid momentous political events. In fact Lezama's work exists against the specific backdrop of not only the Machado and Batista eras but also of the Cuban Revolution of 1959. Since a thorough bibliography is available that documents the studies addressed to Lezama and his political context, I wish only to highlight his general situation, particularly in those areas that proved to be relevant.[11] There are, of course, those who consider Lezama the victim of a Marxist regime. Likewise, there are those who maintain that he was not at all opposed to the Revolution and, to the contrary, was widely published and enjoyed increasing fame during that period.[12] Perhaps the truth consists of arguments from both sides. A consensus of some kind is welcome, if for no other reason than to accurately situate Lezama's work and consider the nature of his political inclinations.

Clearly, Lezama was enthusiastic toward the Revolution during 1959 and the early 1960s. His essays throughout the 1960s heralded the Revolution as the triumph of Cuba's finest aspirations.[13] Still, his enthusiasm was tempered early on by attacks from *Lunes de Revolución,* a literary supplement to the newspaper *Revolución.*[14] In 1961 *Lunes de Revolución* was discontinued, and some of Lezama's detractors either went into exile or remained silent.[15] In 1962 Lezama was named one of six vice-presidents of the newly created Union of Writers and Artists of Cuba, whose president was the poet Nicolás Guillén.

When Lezama published *Paradiso* in 1966, a controversy ensued that prompted government officials to block distribution temporarily (ostensibly because of its explicit homosexual scenes). Yet the novel soon reappeared in bookstores.[16] *Paradiso,* and the controversy surrounding its distribution, greatly enhanced Lezama's reputation. However, between Lezama and officialdom there was eventually a serious clash, which originated with the "Padilla Affair" of 1968–71.[17] This story has been dealt with many times over. As far as Lezama is concerned, its most important element is Padilla's retraction of his antigovernment stance, a retraction that named Lezama as a fellow counterrevolutionary. This accusation was denied by Lezama and his friends.[18] Still, Lezama was never again asked to contribute to Cuba's journals and was denied permission to participate in international congresses.[19]

Despite the negative cast of the controversy over *Paradiso* and the "Padilla Affair," it is not likely that Lezama basically opposed the Revolution.[20] One thing is certain: Lezama never expressed any public criticism, though he often complained of the Cuban establishment in his private correspondence with his sister. Whatever the truth of the matter, there was de facto censorship in his exclusion from Cuban journals and the denial of travel permits, government actions that are remembered in a negative light. Nevertheless, in 1976 (the year of Lezama's death), with the creation of the Ministry of Culture under Armando Hart Dávalos, Cuba began to relax cultural constraints.

Since the end of the seventies, Cuba has witnessed a growing interest in Lezama's work. New editions of his writing are being promoted; critical studies are encouraged; and his home has been designated as a cultural center (it is often the site of lectures dealing with his work). Aside from political considerations, the promotion of Lezama's works in Cuba can be explained by the enormous attractiveness of his metaphoric language and poetic system. This persistent influence is felt not only in many of his old admirers but also among the young Cuban poets.

Chapter 1

Rhapsody for an Absent Nature

The difficulty of Lezama Lima's texts, a fundamental and deliberate element of his work, often invites varied and often contradictory interpretations. Lezama insists that the obscure and the difficult strike us in such a way that "we are awakened by the nature of their distance and difference."[1] To penetrate what we do not understand, he is convinced, is to contribute to the progressive history of knowledge. For this reason, Lezama's metaphor delights in the strange and the exceptional. Far from limiting itself to a cosmetic role, it claims to be the foundation of all reality, a thought implying that "common" language is based on a process of comparisons. Lezama considers the metaphor's "excessive" qualities as the reflection of the characteristics of the Image. For Lezama, the Image is the potential power of the possible, of what has not yet been created: *a creative power stemming from a fundamental absence of natural order.*

The Lezamian metaphor intends to make finite what is invisible and infinite. For Lezama, metaphors are not discoveries of what already exists but are a human medium employed to seize the infinite. He holds no faith in a language that simply reproduces the intelligible world or the natural world. According to Lezama, the so-called laws of Nature are in a constant state of flux. His idea of poetry then implies instability, dynamism, and progressive change. Metaphor is not the reproduction of a world but the creation of a world. Thus the obscure in a poem, far from being an obstacle, is a necessary incitement, an invitation to the unknown. "Actually," says Lezama, "the problem of understanding, or lack of understanding, is an irrelevancy when evaluating artistic expression."*[2]

It is helpful to contrast Lezama's poetic vision with the views on art that the Cuban Jorge Mañach (1898–1961) expounded in public debate with Lezama in 1949. This exercise is intended to demonstrate the rationale behind Lezama's deliberately difficult texts and to emphasize the opposing world views of Mañach and Lezama. The debate signals far more than a generational conflict

---

* "En realidad, entender o no entender carecen de vivencia en la valoración de la expresión artística."

among Cuban intellectuals, for it establishes a basic point of radical departure for contesting cosmologies.

Mañach begins the argument by publishing an "open letter" in *Bohemia* (25 September 1949) entitled "El arcano de cierta poesía nueva. Carta abierta al poeta José Lezama Lima." This article is a response to Lezama, who had sent his book of poems *The Fixity* (*La fijeza*) to Mañach with a note criticizing the indifference of the latter toward Lezama and his magazine *Orígenes*. On 2 October Lezama publishes "Respuesta y nuevas interrogaciones. Carta abierta a Jorge Mañach," his answer to the article by Mañach. Mañach, in turn, writes a second article (published 16 October) in which he sets out carefully to define his ideas about poetry. It is entitled "Reacciones a un diálogo literario (Algo más sobre poesía vieja y nueva)."

In his first article, Mañach reminds his readers of his participation in the avant-garde magazine *Avance*. He expresses his satisfaction with having contributed to the achievements of that journal, but he also confesses his discomfort with the "excesses" of the avant-garde of the 1920s and 1930s. He is particularly uncomfortable with the Lezamian hermeticism, which he views as a return to the avant-garde style. Mañach concludes by noting that now, in 1949, he prefers a style more "direct" and "communicative" than purely "expressive." He defends his preference for a "representative art" by admitting that even during the *Avance* years his "remnant classicism" made him long for "an orderly expression that could offer both clarity and profundity." He emphasizes his opposition to the avant-garde excess of *Avance*, which had brought about the aesthetics of "the ugly and the unintelligible." Here Mañach renounces his own participation in an aesthetics favoring art as "pure expression" and poetry as "no more than a magic irradiation of images and words" (p. 78). On the other hand, since Mañach considers Lezama as no more than an example of the avant-garde, he criticizes him for having forgotten his debt to *Avance*. Clearly, he reproaches Lezama on two counts. First, he has learned nothing from the avant-garde mistakes of *Avance* and has continued to be *vanguardista*. Second, he does not acknowledge his debt to the original avant-garde aesthetics of *Avance*.

Mañach notes in his first article that Lezamian aesthetics seems to be forged in the "visceral," too much a thing of individual gut feelings and far from the attitudes and perceptions shared by the many. Yet despite his violent rejection of what he calls "obscurantist" aesthetics, Mañach concedes that such poetry "is similar, there is no denying it, to what still appears in magazines given over to the work of many famous foreign writers" (p. 78). This observation implies that Lezama's aesthetics is not as isolated as Mañach would like to believe. By noting this, he is undermining his own argument against Lezama.

In his response, Lezama denies any affiliation with *Avance* and adds that many of the finest current writers—Saint-John Perse, Santayana, Eliot, and others—publish their work in *Orígenes*. A free translation of Lezama's argument is as follows:

> We cannot identify, my dear Mañach, with cultural landscapes that did not deliver to our generation any works of decisive character. Their involvement lay with journalism and the mundane world of pragmatic politics. The young writer has not found examples of true artists, such as Alfonso Reyes in Mexico or Martínez Estrada and Borges in Argentina, committed to a Work. There are those among us who refuse to recognize that their prestige is built on a foundation of excrement. They therefore remain insensitive to intellectual and artistic pursuits.*

Mañach insists in his first article that in every age poetry finds a way to communicate in terms relevant to the "common experience" and the "common tongue." In addition, he explains how "individual poetics, stemming from the rebellion of romanticism, has progressively ignored the majority opinion of our times and wrapped itself in the excesses of Sibylline expres-

---

* "No podíamos mostrar filiación, mi querido Mañach, con hombres y paisajes que ya no tenían para las siguientes generaciones la fascinación de la entrega decisiva a una obra y que sobrenadaban en las vastas demostraciones del periodismo o en la ganga mundana de la política positiva. No era, como en México, con el caso ejemplar de Alfonso Reyes, o en la Argentina, con Martínez Estrada o Borges, donde la gente más bisoña, se encontraba, cualquiera que fuese la valoración final de sus obras, con decisiones y ejemplos rendidos al fervor de una Obra. Muchos entre nosotros, no han querido comprender que habían adquirido la *sede* por la *fede* y que están dañados para perseguirse del espejo del intelecto o de lo sensible" (p. 77).

sion, leaving the poet almost entirely alone with his mystery" (p. 90). This declaration states that for Mañach modern poetry since romanticism has evolved in a manner contrary to what he might have preferred. This poetry, time and again, proved increasingly distasteful since it seemed progressively marginal as regards "the common language of the many" in established society. He proposes a return to the order accepted by bourgeois realism with its "representative art." Mañach prefers a poet who does not go beyond the limits but "illuminates" and "ennobles" the majority opinion. One cannot help but conclude that such a solution to the problems of communication places Mañach solidly in agreement with the bourgeois realism of his time.

In his second article, Mañach so thoroughly defines his concept of poetry (p. 107) that the article may well be his most definitive aesthetic statement. The article centers on his specific attack on the avant-garde. Here Mañach demonstrates an overlapping of romantic, classical, realist, and positivist ideas. Although he mentions the importance of the new and experimental in poetry (an echo of his avant-garde days), Mañach is actually developing his idea that poetry must communicate pragmatically and efficiently. This attitude relates his aesthetics with what we can call "nineteenth-century realism." For Mañach, poets must never forget their obligation to express emotions clearly and directly, to write a poetry "that can be understood." Moreover, Mañach defines poetry as no more than "condensed expression" conveying an "emotional experience" through the medium of language. Poets are those who have the necessary skills to express the tensions that have moved them deeply. Poetry is thus a therapy, a catharsis, a spiritual bloodletting (p. 107). Thus Mañach identifies with a kind of psychological romanticism that values poetry for its therapeutic effect. He affirms the basic romantic precept, which holds that the substance of poetry is an array of emotions not subject to any essential change. His insistence on the emotions as the substance of poetry notwithstanding, Mañach also argues for the classical division of the poetic into categories of lyric, epic, descriptive, and philosophical poetry. He is critical of the tendency in modern aesthetics to "not know, or negate, this classical division." In fact Mañach believes that "great poetry" is achieved when expression is so condensed that it permits no addition or deletion.

This sense of "perfect balance" connects his ideas with the fundamental principles of classicism (p. 107).

In contrast, when Lezama, following Pascal, insists that everything can be considered Nature since true Nature has been lost, he is situating himself outside the classical frame, especially as regards the classical relationship of subject and Nature. In this relationship it is imperative that the poet use metaphors drawn from the harmonic balance of "natural" elements. The imagination cannot exceed the limits of the ordinary. Further, the imagination must limit itself in order not to disrupt the classical *decorum* that dictates the typical and universal. Verisimilitude is derived solely from the typical and the general, and not from the strange and exceptional. To achieve poetry from the exceptional, one must consider romanticism as a point of departure.

Mañach reinforces his tendency toward the classical when he accuses Lezama of writing a poetry that ignores the classical frame and "goes beyond the limits." Lezama's answer suggests how strongly he identifies with the "excessive" orientation of contemporary art:

Almost all art and most of contemporary philosophy take their investigations beyond the margins, the wall, or the limitations of causal logic. *For me, the outline escapes me,* said Cézanne, insisting on building what has become for artists an epic of plastic arts. Dostoevsky, Claudel, Proust, and Joyce are among those who have carried the art of language to outrageous possibilities. Isn't it out there, beyond the limits, that we find their darts and insinuations? And isn't it precisely their fury against the boundaries, against the language and situations already made fixed and sterile by the bourgeois perspective, that we find the most fertile fruition for a vision eager to see things as if for the first time?*

Mañach then mistakenly attributes to Lezama an "extreme subjectivity" and places him in the mainstream of individual and subjective romanticism. Ironically, this evaluation is far more appropriate for Mañach's own ideas. Granted that, from a

---

* "Casi todo el arte y gran parte de la filosofía contemporánea, llevan sus problemas más allá del contorno, del muro o de las limitaciones de la lógica causalista. *El contorno me huye,* decía Cezanne, obstinándose en

certain perspective, the relationship Lezama expounds between metaphor and Image is similar to romantic conceptions. Yet essential differences exist. Classical authors, specifically Aristotle, perceive of metaphor as something added to common language, something "extra" that might be superimposed on common language. The effect of metaphor—used correctly—is to combine the familiar with the unfamiliar in a way that achieves grace, distinction, and clarity.[3] At this point, one must recall that Mañach, in his first article, insists that good poetry is characterized by clarity. This is exactly the opposite of the Lezamian vision, which holds that the function of the metaphor has little to do with bestowing grace, distinction, and clarity and is more concerned with the creation of a *new* relationship between elements that were previously unrelated.

For Lezama, the metaphor is an integral part of language, in fact the fundamental part. According to Aristotle, the principal objective of language is to be "transparent," to express as clearly as possible the "naked facts" of reality. Rejecting Aristotle, Lezama does not believe in "naked facts" or in language as an entity distinct from "things" or the "world." For Lezama, both language and the world are assimilated by a constantly changing and transcending metaphor. Aristotle's concepts imply that reality is unchanging, that the metaphor is only part of a learning process, revealing what has always existed. Yet to a modern reader, even Aristole's term "naked facts" is a metaphor. Aristotle's followers reaffirmed, in various ways, his concept of metaphor as an effect obtained through language by the mastery of special forms and techniques. For them, metaphor was no more than a cosmetic, part of the continuing aggregate called "common language." Thus classical rhetoric avoided the relations that involved the strange and the obscure.[4] Metaphor was limited to continuing the sense of decorum and harmony that informed the relationship of its ele-

---

construir la que ha sido para los artistas posteriores una épica de la plástica. Dostovesky, Claudel, Proust, Joyce, y todos los que se han afanado en llevar el lenguaje a inauditas posibilidades. ¿No es más allá del límite donde han situado sus flechazos e insinuaciones? ¿Y no es precisamente en su furia contra el límite, contra el lenguaje o situaciones ya enquistadas por un tratamiento burgués, donde encontramos la mayor fruición para el intelecto voluptuoso de la primera mirada?" ("Respuesta," p. 77).

ments. It is precisely at this point that the aesthetics of Lezama departs from the classical frame.

Just as neoclassical poetry has sought to reveal the harmony of an idealized Nature, many poets in the romantic tradition have explored the sense of hidden harmony that pervades the supernatural, the mysterious, or the exceptional. Although one element of the romantic tradition has certainly exalted personal emotion over universal Reason, other developments in modern poetics have transcended the solely confessional and purely emotional. Lezama assimilates these elements into what he calls the "great symbolist tradition," a tradition that favors the imagination over individual emotion. This symbolist tradition explores the power of creation, of participation in the limitless possibilities of the empty space left by an absence of a natural order.

If the neoclassicists seek their foundation in Ideal Nature, the romantics center their search on an Intimate Self. Lezama surpasses both by seeking the "Image of the *Supranatural*" ("la Imagen de la Sobrenaturaleza"). Lezama's Image is not the product of individual genius. Poetry for Lezama is the possibility of endless combinations, and the poet is the one who captures in the mirror of metaphor a fragment of the fundamental Image. The Lezamian metaphor presents to the visible world an indication of the limitless possibilities of the Image. The strangeness and difficulty of his writing—characteristics shared by much modern poetry—are derived from the modern situation: his metaphors are unique since they attempt to create from the previously uncreated, from what, until now, existed only as potential. These innovative metaphors appear during a modern, fragmented epoch, which lacks a consensus of order and truth. Lezama's metaphor penetrates a primitive universe and generates a language of myth in a time of criticism. The result is a sense of wonder and alienation.

Contemporary poets, like primitive people, do more than simply "represent" symbols and "imitate" Nature. They create symbols and Nature as early people created fables and myths, in an attempt to confer meaning on the chaos of their world. Thus there is a similarity between Lezama and those romantics, especially Coleridge, who rediscovered Vico. Vico had suggested that our first ancestors possessed a poetic instinct, or *poetic wisdom*, which evolved from a fundamental metaphoric sense.

For him, metaphor was the process that created meaning out of the meaningless. Since he neither recognized a static *logos* nor the possibility of an unvarying language, he believed that to invent reality was to create a new reality.[5] Along the same line, Lezama's metaphors intend to create a new reality that has no given organic connections. This "reality" derives from the unique combinations drawn from the productive power of an absence of natural order. Thus Lezama believes that the obscure and the unknown hold the key to those relationships that the poet can bring to light through the process of metaphor.

Lezama's poetry shares the element of primitivism with certain modern poets. Shelley in particular held that the poetic impulse was intimately related to the origin of humanity. He believed that in society's infancy language was inherently metaphoric and every author was a poet. Thus, before the weight of convention established itself, poets had no choice but to speak in a language of new relationships. By this process, the meaning of the world was made increasingly visible.[6] Primitive metaphor is closely related to Lezama's sense of language in a poetic universe constantly replenishing itself. For Lezama, the poet's world is always beginning. Lezama relies on a kind of primitive innocence: the rich world of fable, myth, and metaphor. He believes that a modern poet with a primitive sensibility thinks in a metaphoric way since metaphor is the trademark of the origin of language.[7] The world is thus understood through a series of comparisons and substitutions.

Lezama takes into account Coleridge's definition of language as an instrument of the individual imagination that seeks to capture something beyond the tangible world.[8] He then takes this process a step further and brings his metaphors to life through their intimacy with the Image. For Lezama, the subjective romantic imagination should give way to a more comprehensive vision. The poet must participate in the universal power of constant creation, thus becoming the instrument of expression for possibilities yet unformed in the void of an absent Nature. Lezama's metaphor is the finite expression of the infinite in the Image. Yet his Image is not to be confused with the "images" of the Spanish-American *modernistas* or the French Parnassians who emphasized the physical description of the natural world. His is an Image of the reality of the *supranatural*, a term I favor over "supernatural" since *sobrenaturaleza* has a special meaning for Lezama. Lezama's Image becomes visible through comparisons established by the metaphor. This is a process that announces a new order intended to echo a moment of total creation.

Lezama's metaphor is not the representation of "the concrete" or the imaging of a thought but more akin to a web that draws together fragments of the universal Image. Moreover, since this Image is nothing less than the infinite possibility of creative power, poetry functions as the instrument for shaping patterns from previously irreconcilable elements. This view of poetry has certain affinities with Wallace Stevens's idea of a Nature which embraces and dissolves differences, and these differences are resolved by the similarities established through metaphor. The search for unity among the seemingly irreconcilable is the basic impulse of poetry and language, as well as most human activity. For Lezama, this impulse is behind the exploration and creation of all reality. In fact, for him, this tendency toward affinities is a fundamental direction governing the possibilities of desire itself, a dazzling portrayal of the depth and variety of passion. Thus Lezama's metaphorical process is the key to not only a new aesthetic basis but also to a fresh, engaging consideration of the ethical and the erotic. In addition, Lezama's universe assimilates the modern vision of a language and a world that are basically metaphorical and that progress toward greater and greater expansion. Therefore the contemporary poet always pushes his or her culture to the frontiers of reality and becomes involved in an ongoing process of growth and exploration. Language articulates a new reality and becomes what it articulates. This "new" language is drawn from the vacuum of a lost Nature.

The primary function of Lezama's metaphor is to amplify reality through language, since language is a form of reality. However, unlike some other modern viewpoints, Lezama's involves the *supranatural* as opposed to the subjective sense of metaphor and image. Lezama manages a twist on what Meyer Abrams considers the basic romantic formula: Abrams believes that romanticism attempts to make natural the supernatural, to secularize the supernatural elements of Christianity.[9] In a certain way, Lezama turns this romantic objective and makes *supranatural* the natural. More important, he postulates the *supranatural* as a new reality that fills the vacuum left by the absence of a natural order.

This new reality, this *Supranature*, is the all-encompassing Image that the poet attempts to reveal through metaphors. At the same time, this Image is the substance of creative power that permits the poet to make this revelation.

Lezama insists that his metaphor is not involved with transformation so much as transfiguration. Therefore its principal concern is not the transference of one form to another but the transfiguration, or transcendence, of a form beyond the limits of the natural. In this manner, Lezama surpasses the contemporary idea of language and metaphor as mere transformations between systems of signification. Some modern theories—structuralism in particular—situate human beings in a linguistic context that determines their perception of the world. Language "creates" reality in its own image. To the contrary, Lezama holds that it is the Image that assumes the basic function of giving meaning to the world and permits the creativity of language.

This anticlassicist stance situates Lezama in opposition to a Spanish-American tradition started by Andrés Bello. Bello, in his "Address to Poetry" ("Alocución a la poesía"), stated that poetry should imitate American geography (or Nature in America). If we put aside for now the American aspect—which will be considered in chapter 5—Bello's imitation of Nature corresponds to a poetics that intends to idealize Nature. Nature is thus the source of poetry by virtue of its perfection. From this perspective, poetry aims to overcome imperfection, contingency, and change. The *logos* is an idealized Nature disclosed by reference to the typical and universal. Bello finds Nature in harmony with Reason and worthy of imitation. "Address to Poetry" also suggests a return to the rural, with a corresponding rejection of the urban. The city, as a human creation, is artificial and corrupt. Conversely, Nature not only is uncorrupted but possesses the characteristic of "natural" harmony.[10] Lezama, contrary to Bello, adopts the city as the metaphor of history (see chapter 5). Within the context of the urban, the potential of the Image takes shape.

The poetics of Bello's "Address" is very different from José María Heredia's "Renouncing Poetry" ("Renunciando a la poesía"), a sonnet written in 1823, the same year as the publication of Bello's "Address."[11] In "Renouncing Poetry" Heredia states his frustration with the inability of poetry to overcome contingency and sorrow. This sonnet does not presume to imitate

Nature but instead speaks for a broken poetic harmony. For Heredia, poetic harmony has been interrupted, and he calls this interruption a "broken lyre" ("lira rota"). He can no longer sing the neoclassical concepts of love, virtue, and harmony.[12] Heredia, as poet, believes something is amiss and experiences not only a sense of loss but the inability to articulate the object of his vision. As the first romantic poetry in Spanish, Heredia's is the subjective, intimate song of the "I" overwhelmed by conflicting emotions in a disordered universe. Reason has been overwhelmed by sentiment and imagination. The romantic poet faces a universe of abundant meaning, which the rational tradition is unable to assimilate. The poet's concern is to express the disharmony between deep personal desires and an idealized external reality. Heredia's subject is marked by contradictory sentiments, and Heredia's poetry is not an instrument of universal harmony but the expression of a progressively alienated self. The poet ends up recording a vacuum, an absence, and poetry becomes a progressive rebellion against an empty social and linguistic order. This romantic vacuum is the origin of the absent Nature proposed by contemporary poets like Lezama.

The alienation of the modern poet denies that the true and the authentic can be found in the visible and, in turn, rejects the social and linguistic order of utilitarianism. Yet it is clear that modern poetry is contradictory, both rejecting and accepting modern society. Despite its rebellion, romantic individualism is very much a part of the bourgeois perspective.[13] The world is now the world of "my" experience, and everything is seen from "my" perspective. This is a subjectivity that provokes serious doubt regarding the objectivity of the senses. A clear rejection of empiricism is implied, as well as a recreation of a baroque aesthetics that claims "our senses deceive us" and "life is a dream." The romantic poet attempts to transcend the visible world in searching for the intimate essence beyond appearances. And, as has often been recognized, the poet's inevitable frustration lies in the discord between the demands of the infinite and the impossibility of transcending the finite. The attempt to bridge this discord causes the romantics' anguish, which we find in Heredia.

Heredia concerned himself with exceptional, though natural, phenomena. He drew his inspiration from the violence of waterfalls and the irrationality of hurricanes in an attempt to adapt Nature to his deepest impulses. For example, the poet of "In the Teocalli of Cholula" ("En el Teocalli de Cholula") moves from the general to the particular. The only unchanging element is the poetic "I," the pivot around which the landscape fragments and vanishes. We witness a Nature that, little by little, joins with the darkness of the afternoon until it takes on the aspect of a dream. Here is a Nature adapted to the irrational and the unknown. Heredia's meditation in the presence of the Teocalli suggests the possibility that not only civilizations but also natural phenomena die or, at least, change beyond recognition, leaving only the constant "I" of the poet.[14] This highly individualistic expression of the romantic "I" enhances the potential of the metaphoric process and the subjective imagination. Heredia's perspective prepares the way for Lezama's vision of the Image as the source for an ongoing metaphoric process drawn from the nonrational and the unknown.

In Lezama's poetry, metaphors make visible the infinite possibilities of the Image. The poet assimilates fragments of the Image and unites what remains divided. This echoes José Martí's aspiration to create a philosophy centered on the word *universe*—the One in the Diverse—an idea derived from a fundamental romantic postulate: the imagination is that faculty designed to establish similarities among differences. Martí, assimilating both the romantic and the classical, conceived of Nature as perfect. Whatever imperfections might be discerned in Nature stemmed from the "impurity" of the observer.[15] His implication is unavoidable: there exists a finely tuned relation between the imagination, Nature, and the individual.

The romantic imagination implied by Martí is the perception of resemblances that lie behind the seemingly different in Nature. The imagination is similarity, and the metaphorical process is the human faculty by which similarity is perceived. Poetry is thus an expression of the imagination. For the romantic, imagination is a product of individual genius, a concept that differs from Lezama's definition of Image. Far from being an individual faculty of mind, Lezama's Image is the possibility of all combinations that stem from an absence of natural order. This absence is the vacuum that constitutes the "substance" of creative potential. Thus Image is the void that creates everything. In this sense Lezama is more medieval than romantic.

Medieval conceptions can be compared with the romantic by

juxtaposing St. Augustine's *Confessions* and those of Rousseau. St. Augustine emphasized the revelation of a spiritual power beyond Nature. Hence, his principal concern was not the expression of particular sentiments and intentions. In contrast, Rousseau's *Confessions* clearly represent the romantic vision of a subject obsessed with the intimacies of his particular self. For the medieval Christian, personal expression was secondary to a global vision of Christianity. Consequently, privileged metaphors were those that spoke to collective experience. The fundamental metaphor was the world as a book written by God, a text that could never be fully discerned. This text required a system of interpretation. The world was filled with metaphors that sin had obscured but that contained the meaning of the universe. The Christian's role was to interpret those metaphors.[16]

Dante, the model of Lezama's major novel *Paradiso*, proposes to Can Grande della Scala that there are different levels of meaning in the *Divine Comedy*. This prompts an exegesis that intends to discover the meaning of God and that implies a poetic world view that deliberately avoids the personal and the sensual. Attention is directed toward a universal order encompassing all worldly differences.[17] In the same vein, Lezama's sense of Image is the creative power of infinite advancement that characterizes life itself. Lezama's Image is involved with possibility, and the corresponding metaphor is the realization of a fragment or possibility of this Image. Poetry functions precisely as life and yet is a part of life.

In Lezama's poetics, Nature in the classical sense has been supplanted by the *supranatural* Image. The concept of *landscape* comes to mean the "original" and inviting possibility by which a person can interpret his or her environment. There is nothing "natural" per se, but only an imaginary construct of "reality." Still, this construct is not an individualistic fiction but a manifestation of the creative power of the Image. *Landscape* is thus "Nature" mediated by the *supranatural*, a metaphor for an absent Nature that permits a vital, dynamic creativity. This interpretation of *landscape* is an answer to contemporary alienation from both nature and society. Since the emergence of romanticism, interest in landscape has often been motivated by our alienation from Nature. The symbolic structure of modernity has separated us from the natural. We perceive things not so much by their presence as by their absence, and it is precisely this absence that motivates us to embrace them. Lezama's well-known "Ah, that you flee" ("Ah, que tú escapes") is distinct from a romantic metaphor of subject and object because there is no individual desire for the object but rather a creation drawn from the emptiness between Eros and Image.[18] In this manner the Lezamian Image is the power through which we transform our "first" knowledge of the world.

In Spanish-American poetry, the profound separation from a social and natural milieu can be traced from Heredia's "lyre" broken by anguish, through the final stammerings of Huidobro's "Altazor" and the agonized disarticulations of Vallejo. Lezama's sense of the *supranatural* is an attempt to overcome modern alienation. The symbolic structure of modernity distances humans from their universe, denying a sense of community and participation through imitation of the world. Lezama, to the contrary, intends to create the world anew.

Lezama's "Rhapsody for the Mule" ("Rapsodia para el mulo"),*[19] is an example of his *ars poetica*. Nevertheless, his poetic system is not a conceptualization of his poetry. Instead he proposes a poetics where nothing is free of metaphor, nothing is captured by conceptualizing. Therefore the following study of the poetics implied in "Rhapsody for the Mule" is a violation of Lezama's poetic intent, but I believe that this approach is necessary if we are to add to our understanding of Lezama's work.

The basic metaphor of the poem is a mule moving toward the abyss. For Lezama, this "movement toward the abyss" is similar to the poet's hand seeking its *supranatural* counterpart in the darkness of midnight: "The presence of a hand over one's own hand in midnight darkness is interchangeable with the line of mules making their way into the forest, into the dark. I observed them and saw how their implacable strength moves them toward some unknown destiny."[20] This "*unknown* destiny" toward which the mule proceeds figures prominently in the first section of "Rhapsody." The mule, unaware of his mission, will undergo a transmutation that amplifies creative possibility. His destiny is a "destiny against the rock" ("destino frente a la piedra"), which op-

---

* The original Spanish text of "Rhapsody for the Mule," accompanied by an English prose summary of each stanza, appears on pages 30–37; the text of chapter 1 continues on page 38.

Rapsodia para el Mulo

1 Con qué seguro paso el mulo en el abismo.

2 Lento es el mulo. Su misión no siente.
3 Su destino frente a la piedra, piedra que sangra
4 creando la abierta risa en las granadas.
5 Su piel rajada, pequeñísimo triunfo ya en lo oscuro,
6 pequeñísimo fango de alas ciegas.
7 La ceguera, el vidrio y el agua de tus ojos
8 tienen la fuerza de un tendón oculto,
9 y así los inmutables ojos recorriendo
10 lo oscuro progresivo y fugitivo.
11 El espacio de agua comprendido
12 entre sus ojos y el abierto túnel,
13 fija su centro que le faja
14 como la carga de plomo necesaria
15 que viene a caer como el sonido
16 del mulo cayendo en el abismo.

17 Las salvadas alas en el mulo inexistentes,
18 más apuntala su cuerpo en el abismo
19 la faja que le impide la dispersión
20 de la carga de plomo que en la entraña
21 del mulo pesa cayendo en la tierra húmeda
22 de piedras pisadas con un nombre.
23 Seguro, fajado por Dios,
24 entra el poderoso mulo en el abismo.

25 Las sucesivas coronas del desfiladero
26 —van creciendo corona tras corona—
27 y allí en lo alto la carroña
28 de las ancianas aves que en el cuello
29 muestran corona tras corona.

30 Seguir con su paso en el abismo.
31 Él no puede, no crea ni persigue,
32 ni brincan sus ojos
33 ni sus ojos buscan el secuestrado asilo

Rhapsody for the Mule

The mule walks securely along the edge of the abyss.

At this stage, the mule has no sense of purpose, but his cracked hide is a small sign announcing the darkness of the abyss. Also, a small splash of mud on the mule's hide points to his future wings. Moreover, his blind pace, and the glass and water of his eyes imply that he has a special hidden force. He also carries a swaddling, which wraps him like a blanket of heavy lead. For the mule, there is a constant possibility of falling into the abyss.

The swaddling holds the mule securely to the edge of the abyss and prevents his fall. Also, the swaddling compresses the mule's guts in such a way that his paces produce certain kinds of transformations of the stepped-on rocks.

As the mule descends into the abyss, the successive levels of pathways grow above him.

In his descent, the mule cannot feel, create, or love. Furthermore, he does not look up to seek refuge

34   al borde preñado de la tierra.
35   No crea, eso es tal vez decir:
36   ¿No siente, no ama ni pregunta?
37   El amor traído a la traición de alas sonrosadas,
38   infantil en su oscura caracola.
39   Su amor a los cuatro signos
40   del desfiladero, a las sucesivas coronas
41   en que asciende vidrioso, cegato,
42   como un oscuro cuerpo hinchado
43   por el agua de los orígenes,
44   no la de la redención y los perfumes.
45   Paso es el paso del mulo en el abismo.

46   Su don ya no es estéril: su creación
47   la segura marcha en el abismo.
48   Amigo del desfiladero, la profunda
49   hinchazón del plomo dilata sus carrillos.
50   Sus ojos soportan cajas de agua
51   y el jugo de sus ojos
52   —sus sucias lágrimas—
53   son de la redención ofrenda altiva.
54   Entontado el ojo del mulo en el abismo
55   sigue en lo oscuro con sus cuatro signos.
56   Peldaños de agua soportan sus ojos,
57   pero ya frente al mar
58   la ola retrocede como el cuerpo volteado
59   en el instante de la muerte súbita.
60   Hinchado está el mulo, valerosa hinchazón
61   que le lleva a caer hinchado en el abismo.
62   Sentado en el ojo del mulo,
63   vidrioso, cegato, el abismo
64   lentamente repasa su invisible.
65   En el sentado abismo,
66   paso a paso, sólo se oyen,
67   las preguntas que el mulo
68   va dejando caer sobre la piedra al fuego.

69   Son ya los cuatro signos
70   con que se asienta su fajado cuerpo
71   sobre el serpentín de calcinadas piedras.
72   Cuando se adentra más en el abismo

in the fertile earth. At this point, he is still uncreative, but signs indicate that his condition will change.

Here the mule is no longer sterile: his secure pace in the abyss is his creation. Now he is at one with the abyss. The mule's tears are important offerings toward creativity, but he still cannot see, and he continues in darkness. Suddenly, the mule is swollen and slips from the pathway into the abyss. From the bottom of the abyss one can only hear the mule's questions falling with the rocks into the fire.

The mule's body lies across the burning stones. The deeper the mule falls into the abyss,

73 la piel le tiembla cual si fuesen clavos
74 las rápidas preguntas que rebotan.
75 En el abismo sólo el paso del mulo.
76 Sus cuatro ojos de húmeda yesca
77 sobre la piedra envuelven rápidas miradas.
78 Los cuatro pies, los cuatro signos
79 maniatados revierten en las piedras.
80 El remolino de chispas sólo impide
81 seguir la misma aventura en la costumbre.
82 Ya se acostumbra, colcha del mulo,
83 a estar clavado en lo oscuro sucesivo;
84 a caer sobre la tierra hinchado
85 de aguas nocturnas y pacientes lunas.
86 En los ojos del mulo, cajas de agua.
87 Aprieta Dios la faja del mulo
88 y lo hincha de plomo como premio.
89 Cuando el gamo bailarín pellizca el fuego
90 en el desfiladero prosigue el mulo
91 avanzando como las aguas impulsadas
92 por los ojos de los maniatados.
93 Paso es el paso del mulo en el abismo.

94 El sudor manando sobre el casco
95 ablanda la piedra entresacada
96 del fuego no en la vasija educado,
97 sino al centro del tragaluz, oscuro miente.
98 Su paso en la piedra nueva carne
99 formada de un despertar brillante
100 en la cerrada sierra que oscurece.
101 Ya despertado, mágica soga
102 cierra el desfiladero comenzado
103 por hundir sus rodillas vaporosas.
104 Ese seguro paso del mulo en el abismo
105 suele confundirse con los pintados guantes de lo estéril.
106 Suele confundirse con los comienzos
107 de la oscura cabeza negadora.
108 Por ti suele confundirse, descastado vidrioso.
109 Por ti, cadera con lazos charolados
110 que parece decirnos yo no soy y yo no soy,
111 pero que penetra también en las casonas
112 donde la araña hogareña ya no alumbra

the more the questions cause his hide to tremble. The mule's eyes can only scan the stones now. The fiery stones prevent him from continuing his usual path, but he is becoming accustomed to the darkness of the abyss and to falling upon swollen ground. The mule's eyes are still filled with water, and God continues to pressure him. Though the agile deer can touch the fire and run, the mule continues into the abyss at a steady pace.

The mule's sweat falls on his hoof and soothes the fiery rock. With the contact between his sweaty hoof and the fire, the rock is transformed into something new. Nevertheless, the wrong conception that the mule is uncreative persists.

113   y la portátil lámpara traslada
114   de un horror a otro horror.
115   Por ti suele confundirse, tú, vidrio descastado,
116   que paso es el paso del mulo en el abismo.

117   La faja de Dios sigue sirviendo.
118   Así cuando sólo no es chispas, la caída
119   sino una piedra que volteando
120   arroja el sentido como pelado fuego
121   que en la piedra deja sus mordidas intocables.
122   Así contraída la faja, Dios lo quiere,
123   la entraña no revierte sobre el cuerpo,
124   aprieta el gesto posterior a toda muerte.
125   Cuerpo pesado, tu plomada entraña,
126   inencontrada ha sido en el abismo,
127   ya que cayendo, terrible vertical
128   trenzada de luminosos puntos ciegos,
129   aspa volteando incesante oscuro,
130   has puesto en cruz los dos abismos.

131   Tu final no siempre es la vertical de dos abismos.
132   Los ojos del mulo parecen entregar
133   a la entraña del abismo, húmedo árbol.
134   Árbol que no se extiende en canalados verdes
135   sino cerrado como la única voz de los comienzos.
136   Entontado, Dios lo quiere,
137   el mulo sigue transportando en sus ojos
138   Árboles visibles y en sus músculos
139   los árboles que la música han rehusado.
140   Árbol de sombra y árbol de figura
141   han llegado también a la última corona desfilada.
142   La soga hinchada transporta la marea
143   y en el cuello del mulo nadan voces
144   necesarias al pasar del vacío al haz del abismo.

145   Paso es el paso, cajas de aguas, fajado por Dios
146   el poderoso mulo duerme temblando.
147   Con sus ojos sentados y acuosos,
148   al fin el mulo árbol encaja en todo abismo.

God continues to pressure the mule until the mule slips into the abyss. With this sacrifice, God wishes for him a moment that overcomes death. Finally, the body of the mule falls vertically into the abyss. This vertical fall outlines a cross with the horizontal edge of the abyss.

But the aim of the mule is not just to fall into the abyss. His eyes transform the center of the abyss into a tree. This tree is then transformed from a natural tree into a poetic tree.

Now the powerful mule is sleeping, and he continues trembling in his dream. Finally, the mule's watery eyes are able to plant trees in every abyss.

poses him to the commonplace, the inert. Nevertheless, the metaphor of the *rock* is progressively creative and draws its creative resources from the transformations obtained through its encounters with the metaphors of *water* and *fire*. The metaphor speaks of a rock alive with the potential of creation whose transmutations are made possible when the rock is "stepped on." The rock must suffer metaphorical mutation in order to bring forth the fruits of creativity.

The mule is given a "cracked hide," "already a small triumph over the dark," and we witness a preamble that announces the sacrifice necessary for the possibilities of penetration and creativity. The mule's hide is also lightly splotched with the "tiniest mud of blind wings" ("pequeñísimo ... fango de alas ciegas"). Here the "mud" suggests the material from which God made humans, and "blind wings" points to the mule's potential for flight. Both are further indications of creative possibility. For that matter, *wings*, as a leitmotiv, undergoes a series of metaphorical transformations throughout the poem. Yet in lines 72 and 73 our attention is again directed to the mule's hide, which trembles as the mule progresses more deeply into the abyss. This trembling is due to the questions that penetrate like nails ("rebotan como clavos") into the skin. The reader is reminded of Lezama's image, the "cracked hide" that began the poem. The trembling and wounding are metaphors of portent, of future creativity, of the poetic possibilities inherent in something as unfeeling as a mule's hide.

Lines 7 and 8 establish a relationship between *blindness, glass,* and *water,* terms that describe the mule's eyes. These terms are essential to the poem and indeed to Lezama's poetics. Lezama's metaphorical use of blindness is ambiguous and overdetermined, suggesting the lack of corporeal vision and the possibility of a supranatural vision. Paul, who is often mentioned in Lezama's essays, spoke of a faith visible to the eyes of the spirit and not those of the body. Or, there is one of Lezama's favorite phrases from Oedipus: "Oh darkness, my light!" ("Ah oscuridad, mi luz!"). Both these associations are indications that, within Lezama's system, the metaphor of physical blindness carries with it the potential of a more powerful metaphor, that of *supranatural* vision. Inferences are essential for Lezama since in his poetics true Nature has vanished and must be substituted by the world of Image, an invisible world that sustains a faith in life beyond our present "reality."

The relation between *blindness, glass,* and *water* comprises a complex metaphor: *glass* and *water* are metaphors of reflection and transformation, respectively. What is suggested is the possibility of vision in the dark through both the reflected Image and the transformation of the visible into the invisible or vice versa. The relationship possesses the "strength of a hidden tendon" ("la fuerza de un tendón oculto"), the power of the creative within the Image. As indicated by lines 9 and 10, the mule's eyes are able to scan "the progressive yet fugitive dark" ("lo oscuro progresivo y fugitivo") precisely because of the relationship between *blindness, glass,* and *water.* Here Lezama begins to penetrate the "substance" of the Image's invisible world, a "substance" both progressive and fugitive. For Lezama, the Image is in constant progression toward the total creativity of the universe. The Image is also fugitive and continually evasive: it permits only fragments of its potential to be fixed by metaphor. In this sense, *rhapsody* suggests a musical piece composed of fragments from other musical pieces. Lezama's poetry collection *Fragments to Its Magnet (Fragmentos a su imán)* establishes the same metaphorical relationship between fragments and the Image. The Image, by virtue of its infinite nature, is both invisible and fleeting, evading total capture in the visible realm. Only the perception of fragments is possible. Through metaphor the infinite can be made finite.

Lines 11 through 16 deal with *fixity,* an essential metaphor by which the poet holds together the fragments of the Image. These lines present a "watery space" ("espacio de agua") between the abyss and the mule's sight and suggest that the invisible is united with the visible by the metaphor of water, Lezama's metaphor for transformation. This is a space that wraps around the mule "like the burden of necessary lead/which (heavy) begins to slide like the sound/of the mule slipping into the abyss" ("como la carga de plomo necesaria/que viene a caer como el sonido/del mulo cayendo en el abismo"). The water, as a vehicle of transformation, weights the *poet-mule* with the specific gravity of lead, thus permitting his penetration into the black abyss of the Image.

Beginning with line 17 the poet's image of "blind wings" is transformed into "redeemed wings" ("salvadas alas"). Until this moment in the poem the mule had no wings, a metaphorical reference that recalls the circumstance of Lezama's Narcissus (in "Death of Narcissus"—"Muerte de Narciso"—which is analyzed in chapter 2) who "at high tide fled without wings" ("en pleamar fugó sin alas"). This correspondence is a strategy typical of Lezama: a constant restating of the relationship between various myths and metaphors throughout his poems. His is a metaphorical complex that interrelates a Narcissus ecstatic before his reflection in the water, an Icarus who melts his wings striving for the difficult, an Orpheus resurrected from the darkness of hell, and a Christ ascending without wings in order to redeem humankind.

The stanza continues by noting that what "holds together" ("apuntala") the mule's body in the abyss is simply the metaphorical "swaddling" ("faja") with which God has wrapped him. This girdling prevents the dispersion of fragments. Moreover, the mule's "leaden cargo" ("carga de plomo") has centered itself on the mule's entrails ("entrañas"), thus transforming the metaphor of a *heavy load* into a metaphor for *fixity*. Lezama's strategy is to draw additional metaphors from a "primary metaphor" (in this case the "leaden cargo" that refers to the unifying power of the Image).

This skirt of lead falls "to wet, stony ground/which a name has trampled" ("en la tierra húmeda/de piedras pisadas con un nombre") in order to fertilize poetic possibilities. One of these results in the image of the tree blossoming in the stony ground at the heart of the abyss. This is the final metaphor toward which "Rhapsody" leads: the movement from *stone* to *tree*. Another important element is the transformation of "stone" into "wet stony ground/which a name has trampled." This reflects an essay in which Lezama considers Nietzsche's comment that beneath each stone is a name. Lezama takes this to mean that beneath the concrete and inert exist metaphorical possibilities. Poetry is thus the expression of the metaphorical "nature" of the universe. Everything, in order to be understood, must pass through this symbolic process. Moreover, if the comparisons are to make sense of an apparent disarray, they must be founded on Lezama's vision of the Image as a force drawn from the absence of nature. Meaning can only be produced by the constant encounter between metaphor and Image.

The next stanza introduces new metaphorical derivations, especially that of "the wreaths of the abyss" ("coronas del des-filadero"). These "wreaths" imply layers in the abyss. The "wreaths" evolve; in their developments they move closer to the Image. They continue to assimilate all the differences and thus approximate the endlessness of possibilities.

Beginning with line 30, the poem calls attention to a striking characteristic of the mule. By nature of his sterility, he may mistakenly be considered uncreative and incapable of love. Through these questions the poet prevents the reader from seeking the sterility of conventional answers. The text presents strong relationships among the questioner, the creator, and the process of creative love. This love, in order to be creative, must be grasped the moment it is born. Here Lezama is stating one of his favorite themes: the birth of desire and creativity. The mule's love for the abyss remains blind but rises through "successive wreaths" to the Image. The stanza closes with the repetition of the refrain "the mule's pace in the abyss is slow" ("paso es el paso del mulo en el abismo"), a line stressing the almost imperceptible movement of the mule toward the abyss.

In the next stanza an important transformation occurs in the development of the mule: his evolving creativity replaces his former sterility. Since this section stresses the process of transformation, the metaphors of water and fire are privileged. At times the water metaphor appears within closed dimensions ("tins of water"—"cajas de agua"); at other times it flows forth in the form of tears; and yet at other times the metaphor acquires the immensity of the very opening it represents ("sea," "wave").

The more swollen by the waters of transformation the mule becomes, the closer he moves toward the fall into the abyss, toward the fall into the unknown of the Image. The bloating moves him inexorably toward accepting the invitation of the darkness. Beginning with line 62, attention passes from the mule to the abyss itself:

"Seated in the eye of the mule
glassy, dimly lit, the abyss
slowly scans the invisible."*

Here it is the abyss that is seated in the mule's eye; Lezama inverts the attention of the poem in order to emphasize the shifting relationship of the metaphor and the Image. The abyss "reviews the invisible" from the eye of the mule, and from this perspective the poem signals that in this abyss one can only hear the questions of the mule falling "over the rock toward the fire" ("sobre la piedra al fuego"), transforming the sterile into something new. In one sense, this perspective implies a vision that is almost divine, an attempt to put oneself in the position of the invisible. Furthermore, it must be noted that in lines 65 to 68 especially, the mule is the poet-creator who forms questions and is related, metaphorically, to the forces of creation, feeling, and love.

The poem then returns to the perspective of the mule. It suggests, again, that the deeper the mule enters into the abyss, the more his hide trembles. This section also insists on the physical contact of the hoof against the rock. Nevertheless, the rock must boil with the heat of fire and be soothed with water in order to shape the poetry that it holds. The rock may also be thought of as language, which must be worked and manipulated by the poet to become poetry. In addition, the mixing of rock and fire impedes the repetition of the prosaic.

The transformation from the sterile to the creative is the central theme of the stanza (and, in one sense, of the total poem). Here the poem insists that the movement of the mule into the abyss is not a sterile act, despite the fact that the mule is unable to reproduce himself in a physical sense. It is precisely this absence of the "natural" that permits participation in the *supranatural* of the poetic Image. To develop this vision, Lezama privileges the metaphor of the *house*. The "great houses" ("casonas") are lighted with a "portable lamp" ("portátil lámpara") instead of natural lighting, an instance of something beyond the

---

*

"Sentado en el ojo del mulo
vidrioso, cegato, el abismo
lentamente repasa su invisible."

"natural." In this manner the poet has created a new body for the imagination, something to substitute for the lack of a natural order. All that we hold as natural has been transformed metaphorically. It is important to note that Lezama's comparisons establish themselves between the known and the unknown, and therefore such metaphors are basically, and radically, ellipses.

Lines 118 to 121 suggest that the "bites" (or "scars") left by the fire in the rock are analogous to the signs of the writing that remain from the encounter between metaphor and Image. These "bites" are the metaphors themselves, which remain as testimony to the encounter between the finite (stone) and the infinite (pure fire). The poetry of Lezama refers in the final analysis to poetry itself, metaphors refer to the metaphorical process and to its source, the Image.

A key to the metaphorical thrust of the poem appears in lines 125 to 130: the mule's fall into the abyss has shaped it into the form of a cross. This twist suggests that the appearance of a mule has created an intersection between the vertical and the horizontal that will soon be converted into a tree. This final image suggests the transformation of the poet from sterility to creativity. The metaphor of the tree is so rich that it accomplishes Lezama's poetic objective: each metaphor opens onto a richer one.

In the final stanza the mule is "powerful" and "trembles when he sleeps" ("poderoso," "duerme temblando"), yet within this dream his eyes continue to be "watery." This signals the power to transform reality through poetry. Thus the mule becomes a poet by virtue of his excellence, a poet who is able to transform dead writing into poetry, sterile rock into a tree, the vacuum of a lost Nature into the Image.

Summarizing some of the main points of this chapter, we first compared the poetics of Jorge Mañach and José Lezama Lima to elucidate not only the rationale behind the difficulty of reading Lezama's works but also the opposing world views of Mañach and Lezama. Mañach's "realist" posture is contrasted to the "symbolist" stance of Lezama. Mañach advocates a representative art that "can be understood," while Lezama creates a poetry that seeks to penetrate the unknown, a poetry that is not an imitation of a world that can be passively transmitted through language. A static world does not exist for Lezama, and so poetry is a process of knowledge in its own right: it penetrates the world in order to give meaning to the meaningless. For Lezama, the Image is the creative force stemming from a fundamental lack of a natural order. He bases his poetry on the Image of the *supranatural,* which is basically a vacuum that demands a constant exploration of the unknown. This process is achieved through the metaphor, which, by means of similarities, associates terms that previously had no relation to each other. Furthermore, this metaphoric process always leads to an "exceptional" and "excessive" poetry that breaks with the classical concept of harmony in an idealized Nature. Instead of the classical Nature, one finds in Lezama a *Supranature* that emphasizes the excesses and the enigmas of absence. In this way the metaphor becomes the instrument by which poetry strings together fragments of the Image.

Chapter 2

Narcissus in the Language of Cassandra

L ezama's poetic system is based on the Image as a creative potential stemming from an essential lack of
natural order. His poetics is an elaboration of the conception of Image as origin of knowledge. As such, it is
in keeping with both his poetry and his entire way of com-
prehending the world. Image takes precedence over rationality
in the texts of Lezama; it is the very "nature" of poetry and
truth. Poetry is Image, and Image is the "substance" of the
world. In Lezama's view, the human mind comprehends mainly
through images. Reason is simply a residue of images that we
have already experienced. The world of Image is the source of
reality, but it is a world that can only be called forth indirectly
through poetry.

Lezama's system is a complex, deliberate, and radical restate-
ment of Dante's theory of the imagination as found in the third
section of his *Commedia*. Dante's conviction that "poetic fantasy" is the most elevated function of the imagination is demonstrated when, after his series of dreams in the *Commedia*, he is
able to envision an earthly Paradise without the aid of Virgil, a
symbol for human reason. Dante understood that the imagination
was integral not only to poetic vision but also to linguistic expression. Thus he took into account the functions of memory and
language. It is not surprising that, at the close of his *Paradiso*,
Dante the poet has achieved a notable victory over Dante the
philosopher. Moreover, he has elevated the imagination over both
reason and the mystical, a necessary step in the translation of
poetic insight into human terms. Toward the end of his *Paradiso*,
Dante is desperately seeking adequate expressions for his vision, a
realization of the distance between the world of his imagination
and the universe of language. This Dantescan approach, which for
Lezama signals the beginning of the "great symbolist tradition,"
comprises a major contribution to Lezamian poetics.

Similar to the works of Dante, Lezama's poetry is, from a
religious perspective, an attempt to restore some sort of purity to
language—a purity lost as a result of the confusion brought about
by sin. This original language is derived in Christian mythology
from Adam's first verbal response to God and poses a natural relationship between the signifier and the signified, between the
speaker and the listener. From a theological viewpoint, the

proliferation of languages, symbolized by the Tower of Babel, and the subsequent indeterminacy of linguistic signs are the result of the fragmentation and corruption that characterize the millennia after the Fall. From this context it follows that the language governing human interaction is basically flawed, owing to the absence of a common bond. Thus the poet in the Catholic tradition, faced with this inherent error, sets out to recover through poetry the unambiguous language of Grace, even though the poet may be fated to failure by the nature of the task.[1] Lezama's term *lejanía* ("distance") refers to the basic imperfection of human language. To address this flaw, to bridge this distance, he utilizes the resources of the Image, which is the only testament of a lost Paradise. Therefore, Lezama would suggest, the imaginative act is an artifice, an act made possible in the absence of a pure or perfect Nature. Poetic imagination within this context becomes the expression of a *second nature*, which in turn subverts the rational order and recovers the mythic sense that Western rationalism had displaced.

Lezama's theory of the Image can be considered from various perspectives. If, for example, we take perception theory as an encompassing metaphor for Lezama's poetics, we might recall how, when thinking of someone we know, we create his or her image despite that person's absence; or how, when we look out a bright window from a dark room and then suddenly pull the shade, we are left with an image of the light similar to a photo negative. These phenomena of memory and perception are transformed by Lezama into a poetic statement: the poet is enabled by poetic imagination to exercise a special capacity to recall the faint remnants of a lost harmony. From this viewpoint, poetry is the magnetic force that draws together the scattered fragments of the dispersed, original image. Thus, solely through poetic vision is it possible to approach the creative force of the Image that founds reality.

From another angle (and only in part), Lezama's theory of the Image can be considered postmodern, specifically in its concern with many of the issues raised by Nietzsche, Heidegger, and Derrida: to devise an intellectual project that goes beyond the margins of rationalist metaphysics; to privilege poetic discourse over scientific or logical discourse; and to insist that rationalist metaphysics has never achieved the comprehensiveness it claims to have possessed.[2] From this point of view, rationalist metaphysics has revealed itself more and more to be a dissimulation founded upon a system of thought that deliberately avoids any acceptance of the creative power of the poetic Image. Lezama's interest in Vico, Nietzsche, Heidegger, Mallarmé, and others who emphasize poetic thought over conceptual reason, originates from his view that these writers, from their distinct perspectives, indicate important stages in an intellectual current that decidely undermines an ideology based upon rationalist abstraction, realistic representation, and the individual subject. For Lezama, there is no unequivocal conceptual truth to be revealed by philosophical inquiry. The truth is not a logical proposition but something that preexists the exercise of logic.

Heidegger's contrast between traditional scientific methodology and the distinct methodology of those he terms "essential thinkers" such as Nietzsche is particularly relevant to our exposition of Lezama's poetics. Heidegger's characterization of the essential thinker could well be a portrait of Lezama. A positivist scientist, while readily admitting the limits of knowledge, considers the unknown as eventually knowable, i.e., what we as yet do not know. The essential thinker, to the contrary, is concerned directly with the unknown, recognizing that his or her subject may never be known in the scientific or conceptual sense. The positivist asks in order to obtain pragmatic answers; the "thinker" asks in order to discover the "nature" of the act of asking.[3]

Among the many writers who have challenged logocentric tradition, Lezama selects Nietzsche for special attention. At the end of "Introduction to a Poetic System" ("Introducción a un sistema poético"), Lezama compares Nietzsche's treatment of the Dionysian element in Greek thought with his own. Nietzsche insists there was a lack of creative, Dionysian force in Greek sensibility. In Lezama's opinion, Nietzsche is reacting against the Socratic rationalist element that was the basis of eighteenth-century neoclassicism. Yet whether Nietzsche's theories were influenced by his own historical situation, one thing is certain: Lezama found in the Greeks a creative, Dionysian force that resonated profoundly throughout their culture.[4] The contrast between Lezama and Nietzsche is interesting not only for what it reveals of Lezama's sense of Greek culture and his reading of Nietzsche, but also for what it suggests of Lezama's stance toward the rationalist metaphysical system that Nietzsche had tried to undermine. This attempt was based largely on Nietzsche's obsessive preoccupation with the primacy of existence over philosophical abstraction. Yet despite their varying perspectives, both Lezama and Nietzsche arrive at a sense of the individual as creative and as inevitably transcending the personal.[5] Nevertheless, Lezama's subversions take a path different from the existentialism of Nietzsche. Whereas Nietzsche bases his thought on a prerational existential subject, Lezama founds his poetics on a transcendental Image. At this point we must leave Nietzsche and look to Vico for a further elaboration of Lezama's thought.

In addition to the fact that Lezama and Vico held similar views on history, Lezama was attracted to Vico's theories as a model of a philosophy of *universal remembrances*. This philosophy privileges the Image over conceptual logic. Vico's rejection of Cartesian rationalism is a fundamental element in the intellectual movement that subverted rationalist metaphysics.[6] Lezama defines this marginal thought as "the great symbolist current that flows from the powerful Dante to the delightful Mallarmé" and that, of course, includes Vico.[7] Vico was aware of the contradictions of modern thought that progressively blocked attempts to establish a coherent body of knowledge.[8] Lezama, like Vico, valued not only the Image over the concept, but also the mythical over the factual. Philosophical thought in the West is based upon reason and attempts to integrate all experience around the concrete, i.e., that which is perceivable through the senses or the intellect. The dilemma of modern rational thought lies in its insistence that we achieve philosophical understanding through the principle of evidence, concept, or argumentation. Lezama offers an alternative: situated beyond rationalism, Lezama's poetic system posits the Image as the original, independent, and generative power that shapes all reality. His approach differs from both existentialism and phenomenology. Images are not concepts that take poetic form, but must be taken on their own terms. Since Image is what gives meaning to the universe, the purpose of the metaphor in relation to the Image is to shape experience, not simply reflect it.

For Lezama, *being* is constantly *becoming*, and in his poetic system the role of the Image is to overcome the mutations and fragmentations of time. This explains Lezama's affinity for a system such as Taoism: the Tao is considered an expression of the movement from nonbeing to being, from the void to the image; there is a constant drive toward the recovery of mythic sense, a progression toward Image that aspires to fill the vacuum left by the imperfection of the world.[9] It should be noted that in Lezama's poetic system the movement of the Image is always a fluctuation between Image and Absence, thus explaining Lezama's emphasis on certain metaphors from Egyptian mythology, especially those that refer to the tensions between two opposing elements. For example, there are those that refer to the rising and falling of the Nile in the desert, contrasting the black, fertile soil with the red dirt of the desert: "Black earth and red earth, creative or skeletal, respectively, establish themselves as a continuity, wherein the rural man, who depends upon the fertility of the seasons, penetrates, however subtly, the red earth of atonement and death."[*10] However, Egyptian mythology, as contrasted to the Christian or the Orphic, offers no return from this penetration into the mysteries of atonement and death. Horus, the Lord of Life, was forever excluded from the domain of the dead—in other words, the creative force was completely "used up" or "spent" in the world of the dead where everything finally came to rest. The only significant metaphor in Egyptian mythology that addressed some form of communication between the world of the living and the world of the dead was the representation of Osiris, who continued to engender children after his ritual death. In contrast, Lezama insists that Christianity, whose very basis is the embracing of the image of resurrection, is a highly creative mythology opening up the possibilities of life, a "reviving of life in the desert."[11]

At the beginning of "Investigations" ("Exámenes"), Lezama contrasts his interpretation of the Cassandra myth with his meditation on Roger Bacon, the thirteenth-century Franciscan whose thought was a "precursor of experimental method."[12] His discussion concerns both the contrasts and the coincidences between poetry and the early stages of experimental method. We know

---

* "La tierra negra y la tierra roja, la tierra de creación y el esqueleto de tierra, establecen como una región continua donde el hombre de trabajo campestre, que depende de la fertilidad de las estaciones, va casi penetrando invisiblemente en la tierra roja de la expiación y de penetración en la muerte."

Cassandra as the mythological figure who refuses to sacrifice her virginity to Apollo, the symbol of reason and light as well as the antithesis of Dionysus. Cassandra's refusal prompts Apollo to imprison her in a tower, from which she shouts her mysterious prophecies, unheeded. Since then, the task of Cassandra (poetry) has been to decipher the language of the invisible, the fragmented, the reverse of the obvious. Like Cassandra's prophecies, poetry is given here the aspect of a nonrational discourse outside the scope of science. Without a doubt it is a discourse beyond the limits of the rationalist abstractions upon which metaphysical concepts are based. To contrast Roger Bacon with Cassandra is an interesting strategy since Lezama reminds us that Bacon was not only a precursor of experimental method but also a man who integrated magic into the tenets of modern science.

In order to move beyond the merely conceptual, Lezama begins not from the logocentric tradition but from a vision of an Image that assimilates paradox, an Image made from what is yet to exist. So Lezama believes that conceptual literature freezes the temporal fluctuations of becoming, generating a vicious circle that excludes penetration of the unknown. Lezama stresses the assimilating characteristics of the Image such as being-in-nonbeing, similarity-in-difference, substance-in-the-void. The Image is a source of creativity that has the power to engender analogies out of differences. By way of poetry, the Image expresses "the terrible, encompassing remoteness" of existence.[13]

By Lezama's definition, the Image is a constant emanation of the reality of the invisible world, a perspective corresponding to that of St. Paul, who sought to substantiate faith with the substance of the invisible. Since Paul argued a faith that held with life after death, this belief was based on a kind of imaginary reality, life in another dimension that bridged the discontinuity brought about by the death of the "natural" life. From a theological perspective, imagination seems justified as the substance of a reality beyond "natural" death: how might the imagination exist if there were no substance at the center of this nonexistence? Since Lezama's touchstone is this imaginary substance, within his frame of reference the Image is, in effect, the reality of reality. Poetry is the instrument through which the Image is made manifest and therefore the realization of limitless possibility. From this can be derived the meaning of his metaphorical bridges between apparently disparate elements. Poetic language amplifies the scope of meaning, and consequently the poet can better approach the possibilities of total creativity. Thus the perfect poem would, by the nature of its metaphorical turns, encompass the totality of the Image.

To devise a poetic system capable of expressing fragments of the Image's totality, Lezama looks to the Augustinian concept of the *logos spermatikos,* in which each word participates as a particular moment of the Universal Word. When the Greeks held that each beginning was only a memory, they were affirming that all knowledge had always existed. However, Augustine's concept distinguishes between life as a series of remembrances and life as the unfolding of a potential force taking shape as existence. Thus Lezama's aim is not to remember a priviledged beginning, but rather to re-create "beginnings" that will permit a rich yet inconclusive evolution. For Lezama, the Image is a kind of Time that exists prior to Being, though it is difficult to distinguish between these three in Lezama's poetics.

Lezama presents a literature in which language, as a constant movement between metaphors, activates time yet, paradoxically, still participates in the Christian archetype of Time. Thus chronology in the texts of Lezama is neither circular nor linear but takes the form of a spiral, moving both backward to recreate and forward toward total creativity. He considers this progressive spiral movement as a constant transformation of our present reality into a new beginning. From his perspective, the crucial error is to view existence as Being that has been converted into a static form, trapping Time within the confines of Space. Instead, the poem should celebrate the moment prior to logical categories when time and language were one. This creativity establishes new relationships, a movement brought about by denying words their habitual use and utilizing them to explore the nonexistent.

Lezama's poetic investigations of the unknown, on the other hand, contrast more strongly with those of Heidegger, despite some important similarities. Unlike Heidegger, Lezama does not seek what has already been thought. His interest lies in determining the uncreated. Far from attempting to discover some hidden aspect of prior thought—Heidegger's principal aim—Lezama maintains a characteristic reverence for the impenetrable and mysterious. He believes that Heidegger's inclination is toward the *aletheia*, the revelation of concealed Being, whereas his own attitude is to regard poetry as the penetration of the mysterious.[14] All of Lezama's texts are a constant unveiling and veiling at the same time, and this amounts to a recognition beforehand of the impenetrability of the unknown. The nature of Lezama's language, based as it is in the unknown, thwarts any attempt to conceptually express totality. For Heidegger, the poet is the guardian of Being and poetic language the house in which Being lives. Lezama's poet, on the contrary, is the guardian of the mystery of the Image, and poetry is the sacred ground where Image and metaphor meet. Heidegger's contention is that the traditional stance has moved away from exploring the primordial, thus the necessity to subvert or destroy the traditional. On the other hand, the subversion inherent in Lezama's vision of Image is not a destructive force so much as an energy of creative substitution. He makes no attempt to erase the past completely, but rather favors a revitalization of the creative powers of the imagination. Thus Lezama's attitude toward myth: "All will have to be reinvented, stated anew. And the old myths, reappearing in new form, will offer us their magic and their enigma in strange guise. The enlivening fictions of myth are new myths, with new burdens and new terrors."*[15] For Lezama, tradition must be re-created to sustain its vitality; this is the role of poetry.

But if we accept poetic language as the only valid conduit of our traditions, how can these traditions be subverted by the same language? It is clear that a profound revision of Western metaphysics necessarily causes a dilemma: since modern language is often based on rationalistic concepts, it is truly difficult to subvert rationalism by means of language. It is precisely at this point that Lezama's theory of poetry introduces a poetic language that sustains a kind of shifting bridge between metaphorical subversion and imaginary creativity, capable of naming the unnamed and the unnameable. Moreover, poetic language creates from the well of the uncreated, from what as yet does not exist. This notion gives poetry an ontological function: language is not merely the instrument by which an understanding is passed from one person to an-

---

* "Todo tendría que ser reconstruido, invencionado de nuevo, y los viejos mitos, al reaparecer de nuevo, nos ofrecerán sus conjuros y sus enigmas con un rostro desconocido. La ficción de los mitos son nuevos mitos, con nuevos cansancios y terrores."

other (the basis of realism and rationalism), but also a project of "naming" that presents things in a unique and creative context.

Apart from his challenge to abstract rationalism and realism, Lezama attacks the emphasis on the individual subject and the idea of the particular as something distinct from the generic. The Image is a greater reality than an event, the particular, or the individual, all of which derive their reality from the Image. The individual is not essentially different from the genre. Lezama would consider it absurd to think that poetic creation can be derived from an abstraction beginning with the individual, or the particular, especially if one assumes that they possess a prior reality. Poetic reality *is* reality. Poetic expression is not a rhetorical or generic adornment drawn from empirical reality, and its function does not lie in creating analogies for the concrete. Lezama does not consider the particular, or the individual, as distinct from the Image. This attitude explains his rejection of the existentialism of Nietzsche, whom Lezama views as a representative of the "crisis of individualistic capitalism in the 19th century."[16] This assessment serves to distance Lezama from Nietzsche's idea of an omnipotent individual motivated by the will to power as the substance of being. This viewpoint emphasizes also Nietzsche's extreme individualism as a herald to the end of modern subjectivism.

Lezama's subject is a metaphorical construct that is woven into the dynamic forces within a text. It is a kind of baroque Narcissus who constantly searches for himself in his reflection, an eccentric sort who seeks harmony by way of the image. Lezama's treatment of the subject in his poetry suggests the metaphor of *Narcissus interwoven in the language of Cassandra*. This Narcissus sees himself in a perpetual flow of water, able to glimpse only the fleeting image of his unstable being. Likewise, the metaphorical subject discovers its re-creation in the mirror of language. Lezama displays this highly baroque notion throughout his first great poem, "Death of Narcissus."[17]

Lezama's metaphorical subject is a radical step beyond both the romantic's sentimental subject and the *cogito*, the rational Cartesian subject. It is essential to consider Lezama's contribution within the context of a poetic strategy based on a theory of the Image that does not regard the individual subject as the center and origin of language. Whereas the romantic subject sought union with nature (nature thus assuming the role of the "other"), Lezama's Image encompasses both the subject and nature. The "natural" for Lezama has a meaning apart from either the classical or the romantic sense. True nature has been lost and what remains is the Image, embracing everything, even the subject itself. It is precisely because the Image is generated by an absence that it describes a powerful creativity. In Lezama's poetics, nothing is immutable. All reality is Image, and all Image is a process of unfolding that embraces both subject and space. Both of these, in turn, continually transcend themselves.

One of the reasons Lezama rejects Cartesian subjectivism is that it places subject and space in opposition, giving precedence to the former. In Descartes's philosophy, space is always the subject's "other," projecting itself over space and desiring to possess it. Lezama addresses this point in a short essay entitled "Possibility in Gnostic American Space" ("La posibilidad del espacio gnóstico americano"). Recalling Heidegger's objection to Descartes, Lezama notes that "neither does space exist in the subject, nor does the world exist in space."[*18] This Heideggerian meditation is emphasized by Lezama as a consideration of intellectual development since Descartes. Regarding the concepts of space and subject, Lezama also cites Pascal's paradox: "The universe wraps me in space, but I wrap it in thought."[†19] He joins Heidegger and Pascal in opposition to Descartes's sense of the subjective, emphasizing the fallacy of Cartesian space: since it is not in the subject, it cannot be thought.

Lezama proposes a *gnostic space* as an alternative to the relationship of subject and space found in Descartes. He defines gnostic space as " what man looks to as the only and ultimate instrument of configuration and form."[‡20] This space seeks to embody itself in form or metaphor and points toward the unknown by way of what Lezama has named *transfiguring knowledge* ("conocimiento transfiguratorio"). He explains this as a kind of knowing that is not content with the simple transformation of forms, but searches for something in a new dimension. Transfig-

---

* "ni el espacio es en el sujeto, ni el mundo es en el espacio."

† "Por el espacio el universo me abarca, por el pensamiento yo lo abarco."

‡ "un espacio que busca el hombre como único y último instrumento de configuración y forma."

uring knowledge constantly progresses toward greater wisdom. We see here not only an insight into the relation of subject and space, but also the distinction between Heidegger's concept of the human subject as a being-for-death, who exists in order to die, and Lezama's metaphorical subject as a being-for-resurrection, who exists in preparation for a timeless life.[21]

Narcissus, for Lezama, is neither a rational Cartesian subject nor a passionate romantic one, but rather a metaphorical subject forever in search of its own transcendence. He stands in relation to space—gnostic space—by way of the Image. Both subject and space are functions, or creations, of the Image that encompasses them; they are stages of the unfolding of the Image. Thus the Image integrates at the symbolic level what in everyday reality is a meaningless fragment. The Lezamian subject is metaphorical because it always conveys its meaning by pointing to something other than itself, something beyond itself. The metaphorical subject provokes the initial impulse, the "erotic" force, which gives the Image its generating power. However, to avoid becoming narcissistic, this erotic force must free itself from all possessive desires.

Lezama uses the metaphor of Narcissus, his reflection, and the flowing water to demonstrate the relation of "self" and "other," appearance and reality. This relationship is paradoxical in the sense that, on one level, it portrays the subject as a participant in the providential plan of God, while, on another, it exposes the same theological structure to the possibility of error. "Death of Narcissus" is both an assertion and a questioning of the theological allegory of Resurrection. The poetic voice attempts to integrate the letter and the spirit, but actually subverts any established relationships between the subject and its representation. Narcissus cannot understand himself through contemplation, nor can he totally become an image of God. This paradox is produced by the very nature of Lezama's poetic language. While his metaphors deal with a subject always in motion, always fragmenting itself, there is at the same time a persistent sense of the possibility of unity and a return to the essential.

The constant shifting of the image places the subject in an uncertain relationship. The subject wishes to understand itself completely and tries to integrate this knowledge into a sense of total identity, but this attempt always results in some form of "I don't know who I am." The "I" only seems to approach itself in the form of the "other." Moreover, the face of Narcissus, even though it appears to be fixed, is actually reflected onto the fluidity of the river. The person who knows himself (or herself) is not one who believes he or she has found a way of expressing unequivocal truth, but rather the person who realizes that one must search but never find, that this search for the self is a continual pursuit by means of metaphorical discourse. The seeker must further realize that any sense of absolute conceptual knowledge is an illusion.[22] The subject views itself through a nonmimetic language that does not allow direct correspondence between words and things. The arbitrariness of language dictates the necessity for poetry as a remedy for the impossibility of self-representation. In a totally mimetic universe, language would be a great poem and everything would be poetry. This enigmatic nature of language was recognized early on in the Platonic dialogue between Cratylus and Hermogenes. Since that time, a dialectic has existed between a theory of language that establishes a correlation between sound and sense, and one that accepts the arbitrary and conventional nature of linguistic relationships. Modern linguistics leans decidedly toward this latter view. Nevertheless, there has remained among poets an echo of "Cratylism," a search for essential harmony in language.

Both Mallarmé and Valéry, poets of great importance for Lezama, propounded a "Secondary Cratylism" (the phrase is Gérard Genette's,) which holds that language is arbitrary yet can also possess an essential harmonic element. It is the task of poetry to disclose this harmony by means of certain linguistic strategies.[23] Valéry, in particular, chooses to stress a poetics that will create the *illusion* of harmony. Lezama, for his part, posits the regenerative power of the Image—which gives substance to imperfect language. From a religious perspective, Lezama's vision implies that in a language made imperfect by the fall from grace, poetic harmony derives from the *image-of-Paradise*. Likewise, poetry also seeks to express the total harmony in the *image-of-the-Resurrection* at the end of time. Gérard Genette, discussing the Cratylism of Mallarmé and Valéry, suggests that any sense of poetry with a mimetic function may well be the insight of a particular historical moment that already belongs to the past.[24]

Further demonstrating his belief in the mimetic element of

language, Valéry claims that the poet aspires to present "an intimate sense of union between word and spirit." He also maintains that poetry should strive toward a totalizing sense of language, since language is the masterpiece of literary masterpieces. Accordingly, the poet's creativity is stimulated by the imperfection of the poetic instrument; the poet's task is to develop a theoretically perfect language out of an imperfect one.[25] In "Valéry and the Poetic Act" ("El acto poético y Valéry") Lezama questions Valéry's insistence upon language itself as the poetic ideal. He suggests that the emphasis should be placed on the "substance" of poetry, which, for Lezama, is always the Image generating all language.[26] Following what is clearly an unorthodox Catholic poetics, Lezama proposes that instead of considering language as the only instrument capable of multiple associations, perhaps it is necessary to focus attention on the redemptive potential of the metaphorical subject.[27] The poet recovers language from disorder, corruption, and discord caused by original imperfection.

For Lezama, the surest way to a radical frustration is to perceive language as the literary ideal. He rejects Valéry's conception of a linguistic methodology that presumes to reveal the secrets of language and the universe, eliminating ambiguity and obscurity and replacing mystery with mathematical perfection. Taking the human language as his object of investigation, Valéry encounters the paradox of a subject who tries to represent itself in its own discourse. The "I" doing the speaking is the same as, yet distinct from, the "I" represented by the speech. Valéry thus proposes a detailed, intensive examination and probing of those secrets hidden within the "I" who sees the mirror and the "I" who is in the mirror. This scrutiny of "self" and "other" will, according to Valéry, result in a precise knowledge of the basis of language, moving the human subject closer to a synthesis of the two poles.[28] However, Valéry conceives of this synthesis as merely an illusion of harmony. It might be said that Valéry views the ceaseless flux and contingency of time, the fragmentation of existence, as preventing Narcissus from seeing his reflected image clearly. Thus his "First Fragment of Narcissus" is a text that attempts to suspend the motion of time.[29] The waters of the poem are absolutely calm, and the poet hopes to hold in suspension the *élan vital*, even if only the illusion of a synthesis between the object and its reflection is achieved. But since this synthesis is no more than sensory illusion, poetry is eternally frustrated. Unless it can succeed in evading the flux of time, the only stasis it can manage is essentially illusory, since incessant change does not allow for intellectual precision or purity of ideas.

If we compare Valéry's "First Fragment of Narcissus" with Lezama's "Death of Narcissus," we first note that in Lezama's poem it is difficult to determine a clear sense of linear time. The linguistic complexity creates a labyrinth of metaphors that make it difficult to determine a precise chronology. However, this is not to suggest that Lezama's poem addresses the problem of time in a manner similar to that of Valéry. In Lezama, temporal progression is purposely ambiguous. This ambiguity is not sacrificed in order to analyze the truth of language and being in a metaphor of suspended purity. The indeterminacy of "Death of Narcissus" allows a variety of interpretative possibilities: a chronological frame in which Narcissus throws himself into the waters and then is reborn, a series of variations on the death of Narcissus, the metamorphosis of Narcissus into Icarus, the qualitative leap from metamorphosis to transfiguration as Narcissus becomes Christ, and so on. Time, like many of the elements of this poem, sustains a textual richness that permits various options and even contradictions. But with Lezama all these alternatives are always accompanied by the possibility of salvation: the text aspires to the comprehensive totality of the Image at a *supranatural* level. Thus readers of Lezama's poem are confronted with both the aesthetic and the moral, and in the act of reading will find themselves choosing one path or the other. There is no unequivocal moral or aesthetic message other than the existence of a variety of possible directions. This poetic indeterminacy is like the desert metaphor in Dante's *Commedia*: at the same time a place of temptation and a place filled with the hope of salvation.[30]

Time in "Death of Narcissus" is at issue from the first line, as is the mythological association of Narcissus with Danae. The beginning of the poem reads: "Danae weaves golden time by the Nile" ("Dánae teje el tiempo dorado por el Nilo"). In this way, Lezama presents a mythic strategy centered on the issue of temporality. He relates the ancient myth in which Danae is imprisoned by her father as a reaction to the prophecy of Tiresias, who has warned that a child of Danae will kill his own grandfather. Although captive, Danae is covered by a golden rain and conceives

Perseus. Acrisio, her father, expels Danae and Perseus and puts them out to sea, where they are rescued by Seriphos and taken to an island. Later, they return to Greece and the prophecy is fulfilled when Perseus accidentally kills Acrisio. The unfolding of time is implied in this homicidal act. The death of the grandfather at the hand of Perseus is like the death of the father (or the Father in the Freudian sense) at the hand of Oedipus. These parricides are metaphors for Time, which, in order to continue through its changing progressions, must erase the past while at the same time manifest disturbing truths. Lezama's sense of temporality encompasses precisely this paradox: a tradition that remembers, and a parricide that erases, a simultaneous act of memory and forgetfulness.

Thus, as is characteristic of all of Lezama's work, the idea of Time as destructive and parricidal is always accompanied by its counterpart at another level: the idea of salvation, or of a sacred moment. If, on the one hand, the "Death of Narcissus" is involved with the idea of a linear, parricidal chronology, there exists, on the other hand, the possibility of transcending this level and moving to a "higher" plane: that of a successive and sacred mythical Time that feeds precisely from the integration of the Father and not from his death. The Narcissus who throws himself into the water may be considered a suicide or a martyr for the salvation and recuperation of a lost memory.[31] The suicide of Lezama's Narcissus can easily suggest the type of martyrdom that permits the possibility of the rebirth of the "new man" in a deeply Christian sense. Narcissus, as we know, is the son of Cephisus, the river god. Thus the act of throwing himself into the river can be construed as a return to the father. Narcissus, spotting his image reflected in the waters of the river, sees, from one perspective, his image cast upon the shoulders of his own father. This idea can be related to the Lezamian transformation of Narcissus into Christ and his ascension to God the Father.

Regarding the concept of Time, one must also note that the first line of "Death of Narcissus" associates the myth of Danae with the Nile. It is in the flowing waters of a river, a recurrent temporal metaphor in Western literature, that Narcissus first glimpses his image. In his "Introduction to a Poetic System" Lezama writes that "all movement, as such, stems from desire and its initial frustration."*[32] The waters of Time and Being, like a kind of Heraclitian river, flow unceasingly, and from the paradox of constant motion sustained by an unmoving image emerges Lezama's conception of Being that, paradoxically, is always in a state of unfolding. As Lezama explains in "Introduction to a Poetic System": "From this sense of Image, inhabited by both a particular and a universal substance, emerges true Being."† He later adds: "'I am, therefore I exist.' That awareness of the Image exists, that being has an existence as something derived, therefore it exists both as being and as body." Lezama continues: "From man's fear that he is an unruled plurality, that his sense of being is a fragmentary existence, and that even the zone of being is nothing but a fragment, came about what Goethe has termed 'the previously unimagined: a life simultaneously active and at rest.'"‡[33] In this sense, Lezama's Being is an act born of motion, a *derived* Being created by the Image that, in turn, makes itself manifest only through temporal metaphors.

The Image is responsible for the unfolding of Time. Therefore, according to Lezama, Being manifested in Time is fragmentary because it appears as a moment in the process of becoming. Owing to its ongoing fragmentation, it cannot acquire total knowledge of itself or total identity with itself. Movement is, then, a manifestation of the multiplicity of Being. Narcissus can never coincide perfectly with his image since his being and his image are everflowing fragments. To achieve identity would be a kind of death. Following Lezama's thought, poetic discourse exists in the tension between the absolute vacuum of the Image and the analogy of the metaphor. Poetry is a constant interchange between the visible Narcissus, fragmentary and fleeting, and the unseen Image that serves as the source and support for what is seen. Lezama's

---

* "todo movimiento como tal es una apetencia y una frustración inicial."

† "En esa conciencia de ser imagen, habitada de una esencia una y universal surge el ser."

‡ " 'soy, luego existo.' Esa conciencia de la imagen existe, ese ser tiene un existir derivado, luego existe como ser y como cuerpo.... En ese temor del hombre de que es un plural no dominado, de que esa conciencia de ser es un existir como fragmento, y de que fuera quizás un fragmento la zona del ser, surgió en el hombre la posesión de lo que Goethe llama 'lo incontemplable: la vida eternamente activa concebida en reposo.' "

metaphor reaches out to capture the total Image while recognizing the impossibility of this objective at the purely human level. Poetry is an orbit around an absence or essential totality. Whether Narcissus can surpass the anguish of nothingness depends on the degree to which he can integrate his fragmentary self with his original image at a *supranatural* level. With this total integration, Lezama's text hopes to overcome Valéry's *ennui*.

A baroque reading of the myth of Narcissus emphasizes two central motifs: flight and reflection. Here also, though by way of a different focus than that practiced by Valéry, exists the same problem of "self" and "other." The difficulty lies in the fact that Narcissus cannot achieve the clarity that a perfect knowledge would demand: his reflection is "the deceptive firmness of the mirror" ("firmeza mentida del espejo"), while his shadow opens onto an "ever-changing pontiff" ("cambiante pontífice") (p. 653). His is a fugitive image, since the space that provides his reflection is constantly evaporating. The water is always moving, and Narcissus can neither recognize nor love himself without falling victim to the ephemeral. Regarding the reflection itself, it must be noted that it is an ambiguous metaphor: it deals with the "self" and the "other" at the same time. The resultant ambiguity creates the powerful dynamics of the baroque. Narcissus will never know himself completely, and his sense of recognition will always be somewhat fraudulent and deceptive. What Narcissus sees reflected in the water is, simultaneously, his self and his negation.

The ambivalent vision of Narcissus finds an aural counterpart in the mythical figure of Echo. The myths of Narcissus and Echo are closely related, both representing the possibility of sensory imperfection (Narcissus that of vision and Echo that of voice and hearing). Both figures often appear within the same mythic context: Echo is presented as one of the nymphs in love with Narcissus. Furthermore, as one who is never able to obtain the object of her desire, she can merely repeat the last part of what others say. If Narcissus can glimpse nothing more than a fragmentary image, Echo can only imitate an incomplete voice. In "Death of Narcissus" Echo is nowhere mentioned, but her fragmentary voice is often suggested: throughout the poem there exists a continuing relationship between the visual and the aural, between the illusory delineation of the "cold stare" ("fría mirada") and the "pinned tongue" ("lengua alfilereada") of Echo. Stanza V, for example, provides a series of visual images that are deliberately distorted (a reference to the reflection of Narcissus), while a doubled voice interjects itself: "the hand without echo, the pulse unfolded" ("mano era sin eco, pulso desdoblado"). As the poem develops, the visual and aural images gradually overlap until they reach the synesthesia of "green shrieks" ("verdes chillidos"). Synesthesia can be construed here as a metaphorical process leading toward an eventual moment of total creativity in which differences between the senses no longer exist. This merging strategy of the poem suggests the possibility of transformation and salvation.

The baroque motif of the illusory reflection appears throughout Lezama's poem in many guises and implies much of the rich history of the Narcissus myth. As an example, there is the image of the bee, a constant in the Narcissus myth since the beginning of Christianity. In the second century Philostratus published *Eikónes,* a series of descriptions of paintings that examine the correspondence between verbal expression and visual impression. Among his selections, Philostratus described a painting of Narcissus, emphasizing the Ovidian theme of *appearances that deceive.* He begins his discourse by noting that, in much the same way as the pool reflects Narcissus's image, the painting itself represents the pool. Philostratus then describes a few white flowers painted with great realism. These flowers have grown around the edge of the fountain as a result of the metamorphosis of Narcissus. A bee has been painted on one of the flowers, also with great realism. Philostratus maintains that the bee has been victimized by the deceivingly realistic appearance of the flowers, just as an observer of the painting might be fooled into thinking the painted bee is real. This is followed by an exhortation to Narcissus advising him not to be deluded by the illusory image he sees in the water but to meditate instead upon the deception.[34] The bee serves to emphasize even further the fictitious character of the reflection: Narcissus, falling victim to the allure of his own reflection, throws himself into the water and is converted into a flower; a bee, tricked by the realism of the painted flower, approaches to sip its honey; and, finally, the observer of the painting is fooled into thinking the painted bee is real. This game of illusion using the image of the bee is basically the same as the multitude of perspectives appearing in baroque works like *Las Meninas* and *Don Quixote*: the painting within the painting, the book within the book. The bee, in this case, might be considered as the image that can mistakenly induce an observer to believe that what he or she beholds is a tangible reality. And, as might be expected, the theme of the illusory reflection can be associated with the relationship between the subject who writes and the subject's self-representation in his or her writing.

In "Death of Narcissus," the image of the bee first appears in stanza XI, where it seems that Narcissus has thrown himself into the water and is experiencing a rebirth.*[35] The bees appear again in stanza XII, in a line that, through alliteration, connects the image of the bee with that of the mirror: "If you move away, fine *bee*, the mirror destroys the mute river" ("Si se aleja, recta *abeja*, el espejo destruye el río mudo") (p. 656). Finally, the bees are mentioned in the penultimate line of the last stanza, in a context that has been tempered by instances associating Narcissus with Christ: "if he settles himself on his side or toward the front the Centurion batters his rib" ("si se sienta en su borde o en su frente el centurión pulsa en su costado") (p. 658). In the final moment before ascension, when "Narcissus, at high tide, fled without wings" ("Narciso en pleamar fugó sin alas") (p. 658), the bees again appear: "Swarms of uncreated *bees* sting the wake, demand of him the rib" ("Chorro de *abejas* increadas muerden la estela, pídenle el costado") (p. 658). One possible interpretation of the bee is as a symbol of everything fraudulent.

Some versions of Narcissus emphasize the negative qualities of the myth: vanity, arrogance, a distorted perception of reality. However, the German Jesuit Masenius, in his *Speculum imaginum veritates ocultae* (1650), finds something positive within the constellation of negatives.[36] In his brief summary of the myth, he notes that Narcissus fell in love with his reflection and transformed himself into a flower. Masenius explains that the Narcissus figure can represent an excess of self-love and the placing of one's own preferred physical beauty over divine grace. Yet he

---

* Frescas las valvas de la noche y límite airado de las conchas
en su cárcel sin sed se destacan los brazos,
no preguntan corales en estrías de *abejas* y en secretos
confusos despiertan recordando curvos brazos y engaste de la frente
(p. 656).

adds: "he is also an image of the kind God who loved man and became flesh" [my translation—E.B.].*[37] As Masenius demonstrates, the attributes of Narcissus are paradoxical, even contradictory. Both the fallen soul and its savior are represented in the same metaphor: Narcissus in love with his reflection. It is precisely within the tensions and ambiguities inherent in a baroque perspective that Lezama situates his Narcissus.

Another tendency of the baroque is to transform Narcissus into a Narcissus-Christ figure. We find this not only in Masenius's *Speculum* but also in *The Divine Narcissus* of Sor Juana Inés de la Cruz.[38] This play, written in 1685, belongs to the Spanish-American baroque period and is based on a Catholic interpretation of the pagan myth. It is a work in which Sor Juana attempts to reconcile Human Nature with the image, or reflection, of Christ, the Divine Narcissus. Human Nature is led by Grace to the Fountain of Life. Once there, it situates itself in such a way as to cast its reflection over that of Narcissus, who has also approached the Fountain, attracted by the reflected image. Narcissus, in a monologue following closely the laments of his Ovidian counterpart, acknowledges that he is embracing his own image. The play closes with songs of praise to the Incarnation and the Holy Trinity. A sacramental play, the work was written to be presented during the celebration of Corpus Christi and thus has as its central motif the transformation of bread and wine into the body and the blood of Christ. The prologue to *The Divine Narcissus* is a short, dramatic poem of praise that presents a peaceful, agreeable encounter between Indian and Catholic beliefs. Christian, Greek, and Aztec myths are afforded equal footing as the play reinforces the similarity between Christ and the Mexican god of vegetation. Both offered themselves as "food" for the faithful. The purpose of *The Divine Narcissus* is to praise the mysteries of Christian salvation. Lezama looked to this work as one of the founding examples of the integration of Indian and Spanish cultures expressed in the Spanish-American baroque and contrasted it with Calderón's *Echo and Narcissus*.[39] For Lezama, *The Divine Narcissus* was an outstanding work in the literature of the New World. Spanish-American baroque, particularly as exemplified in this work where the gods of the old world and the new are combined and transformed, es-

---

* Masenius: "Est vero etium quaedam imago Dei amore hominum icpati atque incarnati."

tablishes a bridge between European and Indian beliefs. This is a basic, necessary step in the process of what Lezama calls "the American cultural expression" and serves to highlight the importance of a major aspect of "Death of Narcissus." Lezama chooses, as the subject of his first major poem, a Narcissus-Christ figure drawn from the Spanish-American baroque tradition.

Despite their basically different approaches, a common theme of salvation unites all three of the reworkings of the Narcissus myth we have examined. The frigid, unmoving waters of Valéry's poem are intended to suggest that Narcissus, examining his reflection, can arrive at an intellectual grasp of his "self" and his "other"; the Fountain of Life in Sor Juana's play contains the purifying, baptismal water meant to bring Human Nature closer to Grace and, therefore, to the salvation of the Divine Narcissus; and the water where Lezama's Narcissus is reflected is a river of paradoxes that deceives and kills, but also purifies and saves.

"Death of Narcissus" may suggest the Christianization of both the Narcissus and Danae myths. Lezama places Danae in a contextual relationship to the mystery of the Incarnation: as the myth reveals, Zeus covers Danae in the form of a golden rain and engenders Perseus. This basic metaphor represents the classical version (*avant la lettre*) of the Christian Incarnation of the Word: the Holy Spirit in the form of a ray of light descends over the Virgin and engenders the Son of God. However, if Perseus comes into the world to fulfill a prophecy of parricide by finally killing his grandfather, Christ's purpose is to reunite man with the Father. Christ does not kill the Father but rather returns to Him, as Narcissus returns to the river of his father Cephisus. Thus Lezama's poem concerns both the death of Narcissus and the more complex incarnation, death, resurrection, and ascension of Christ. The poem begins with an allusion to the mystery of the Incarnation (by way of reference to the myth of Danae) and closes with an indirect allusion to the mystery of the Ascension ("Narcissus, at high tide, fled without wings"). These descending and ascending movements are defined by Lezama as the *súbito* (suddenness), the instance in which fragments of the Image appear through a metaphor, and the *vivencia oblicua* (indirect experience), the moment when a metaphor tries to grasp a fragment of the Image. This relationship between *súbito* and *vivencia oblicua* traces a constant, decentralized ellipsis that seeks, through the comparative effect of metaphor, the universe of the total Image, a world that Lezama calls the *esferaimagen* (sphereimage).

The text of "Death of Narcissus" is characterized by indeterminacy and polysemy. The sustained enigma of Lezama's poetry is an example of the kind of writing that always achieves something more than, and different from, what it first intended. The poem is a web of interpretation that traps in its strands the voice of the poet, as well as those of others, and holds them in judgment. With this radical questioning, the text undermines the stability of any perspective. In much the same way, the myth makes of Narcissus, the reflection, and the water an exploration of the unstable relationship between "self" and "other." The metaphorical moment of Lezama's text is always suggestive of the possibility that the moral significance of the Image is always falsified by appearances, and that the corruption of time exists between what is expressed and what is meant. Metaphor in "Death of Narcissus"—as, for that matter, in all of Lezama's work—serves to dramatize the internal distance between the signified and the signifier. The very act of the poem—its discourse—occupies the ambiguous space between self-referential and omniscient writing yet without ever achieving either of these possibilities.

The changes in narrative voice in the text of "Death of Narcissus" serve to exemplify the ambivalent relationship between the voice of the poet and that of an incomplete perspective. The poem is almost always voiced from the omniscient perspective of third-person singular. Yet in stanza VI there are two instances of the use of first person: "the fish staring at *me*" ("pez mirándo*me*") and "they always ask *me*" ("siempre *me* preguntan") (p. 654). By this change to first person, the poetic voice descends from an omniscient, morally superior perspective to a full identification with Narcissus (in his guise as transgressor). Both poet and reader are participants in imperfection, inheritors of a basic degradation. The distinction between the first and third person calls attention to a text that dramatizes the debate between an identification with the transgressor and a morally and intellectually superior stance. The suggestion of the potential for the latter is most strongly stated in the exhortation in stanza XV:

Narcissus, Narcissus. The antlers of the murdered deer
are fish, are flames, are flutes, are nibbled fingers.

Narcissus, Narcissus. The Florentine hair forming the
design swirls in profiles. *

From a religious perspective, this exhortation hopes to move the
reader in the direction of moral imperative yet is not itself ex-
empt from the instability of language and cannot escape the ambiguous nature of textuality. The relationship between the first-
person singular and the admonition comes to resemble the dis-
crepancy between a humble pilgrim seeking personal salvation
and the proud voice of the poet. Lezama's text dramatizes the
writing process as an action interwoven with traps and tempta-
tions. Only a flawless Creation could be expressed with a mimetic perfection in which the word and spirit were identical. In
a certain manner, this is the way that Lezama perceives the role
of poetry: as an unceasing act of creation, the embodiment of
the infinite Image in a finite metaphor. This explains the importance of a human being who participates in creation, someone
able to relate the most dissimilar things by means of poetic
language. Lezama says that the human being is "a monster who
throws out questions that have no answers."[40] Hence the need
for the metaphoric process of Lezama's poetry: through his
metaphors, the poet first transmits then amplifies the image of
poetry.

There also exists in "Death of Narcissus" an indication of the
potential of the Image, a sense of direction by which the hetero-
geneity of the various manifestations of being aspire to total union
in what Lezama himself calls the "ecstasy of participation in
homogeneity."[41] Thus Lezama's Image can realize itself histori-
cally through metaphorical expression. This, in turn, becomes the
temporal form that permits a poetry of mediation. Metaphor,
then, subverts not only the established structures of language but
also the structure of what is commonly defined as reality. To ask
if Lezama's metaphors achieve reality is to assume we know what
reality is. But if we assume metaphor can redescribe the world, it
follows that this redefinition is a new reality. Thus Lezama's
discourse serves neither to improve the pragmatics of communica-

---

* Narciso, Narciso. Las astas del ciervo asesinado
  son peces, son llamas, son flautas, son dedos mordisqueados.
  Narciso, Narciso. Los cabellos guiando florentinos reptan perfiles
     (p. 657).

tion nor to aid it in a traditional, conceptual manner. Its purpose is to subvert and expand our vision of the world. This is Lezama's heuristic strategy, aimed at rediscovering reality. Metaphor, as the finite form of the infinite Image, is at the heart of a text that presupposes the transformation of language and reality. If ordinary language strives toward clarity and scientific language aspires to the unequivocal expression, then the objective of Lezama's text is to attempt to express the tension between sameness and difference, to express the sameness in difference. This process generates poetry with the power to penetrate the unknown and to create everything anew. Thus it is that when Lezama creates a metaphor to describe a past event he is re-creating reality, which, since it is never static, must be re-created in the metaphorical process of human memory. Lezama, subverting such fundamental concepts of Western metaphysics as rationalist abstraction, realistic representation, and the individual subject, arrives at a conception founded on the Image, an Image always manifesting itself through metaphor and ever dynamic in its potential for rediscovery, redefinition, and re-creation.

Chapter 3

Salvation through Writing

We have seen that for Lezama poetic knowledge is related to the breaking of limits. Yet "always going beyond established limits" brings with it the danger of deeply fragmenting the human subject and provoking a constant alienation between the poet, language, and the world. Lezama's solution to this paradox is to create a poetics of the Image in which Image assimilates writer, language, and the world within a creative potential residing precisely in the absence of limits, in the vacuum produced by the loss of natural order. For Lezama, the poem is an exceptional act of penetration—therefore an erotic act—into creativity within the fundamental void of the Image. But what lifts Lezama's poetics above the exclusively erotic is his insistence upon a poetry that seeks, then transcends, desire.

The poem participates in a universe that presents to the subject the *rhythm* of desire, thus avoiding an alienation between the creator and his or her creation. This desire, from Lezama's perspective, is not the possessive search for an unattainable object but the memory of the universal rhythm of desire, which is, in sum, the Image. This is precisely the meaning of the metaphor of the young pheasant that Lezama shows in "Investigations" ("Exámenes"), wherein he proposes that the bird's desire stems not from hunger for the food in front of him but from the memory of a rhythm superior to his hunger:

In order for the young pheasant ... to learn how to eat grain, it is not possible to force his neck close to the food. If we take a pencil and begin to tap it, creating a continual rhythm, following the rhythm of the pencil's tapping, the young pheasant begins to eat. How is it possible to finally bring about, to synchronize, his hunger with the rhythm? Is this exercise superior to his hunger? Let us suppose an irregular series of situations: that the rhythm continues but the grain is useless; that the young pheasant, seduced by the rhythm, ingests a deceptive, painted grain, and dies; that after his death the rhythm continues, before another young pheasant. We linger, because of the young pheasant: very few taps of the pencil are sufficient in order to provoke his neck to copy anew this rhythm.*[1]

The theme of desire and rhythm is often expressed by Lezama through various metaphorical strategies. In the poem "Call of the Desirous Man" ("Llamado del deseoso") from *Concealed Adventures* (*Aventuras sigilosas*), the emphasis falls upon a poetic rendering of the relation between a mother and son and the consequences of this relationship in the poetics of desire that characterize the adult male: "Desirous is he who flees the mother," "The depth of desire does not aim toward stealing the fruit./The sting of desire is to shun sight of the mother./It's the absence of the continuity of a day that prolongs itself."†[2] This metaphor of the *desirous man* is similar to that of the *young pheasant* in that both involve the conception that desire is not only brought about by a *lack* but also manages to sustain itself through a *remembered rhythm.* Thus the nexus between the poetic and the erotic in Lezama's *Concealed Adventures* is, perhaps, where such a relationship can be presented in its most dramatic configuration.

Almost all the poems of *Concealed Adventures* suggest anecdotes of exceptional sexual encounters. In fact the entire book is an ellipsis of the sexual act. The metaphors and other rhetorical figures are, then, a kind of fabric within a suppressed world and are symptomatic of concealed desire. The ellipsis, as the rhetorical figure that relates a known term with an unknown one,

---

* "Para que el faisán joven ... aprenda a comer los granos, no es posible acercarle su cuello a ese alimento. Si cogemos un lapicero y vamos punteando, provocando un ritmo continuo, siguiendo el ritmo del lapicero, empieza a picotear los granos. ¿Cómo entrelazar finamente su hambre con un ritmo? ¿Es ese ejercicio superior a su hambre? Supongamos una serie irregular de situaciones. Que el ritmo se prolonga, pero el grano está inservible. Que el faisán, seducido por el ritmo, ingiere un falso grano pintado, y muere. Que después de su muerte el ritmo continúa, frente a otro faisán joven. Detengámonos, por respeto al faisán joven, bastarán muy pocos punteos del lapicero para que su cuello intente remedar de nuevo ese ritmo."

† "Deseoso es aquel que huye de su madre," "La hondura del deseo no va por el secuestro del fruto./Deseoso es dejar de ver a su madre./Es la ausencia del sucedido de un día que se prolonga."

is a frequent recourse throughout the work since there are several veiled references to exceptional erotic situations. For example, in the poem "The Port" ("El puerto"), the erotic theme is introduced with a phrase from Tirso de Molina that refers, implicitly, to the Don Juan myth: "the sea wishes to ask us, *will you dine with me this evening?*" (my emphasis).*[3] From this moment on, all the poems consistently refer to processes related to the sexual act, the vagina, and the phallus. Lezama establishes a series of complex relationships that are connotative of the female sexual organ: "flower," "wagon," "mouth," and so on. The references to the phallus are also numerous: "toad," "rooster," "snout," and so forth. Of the many inferential allusions to the sexual act, the most significant is the one that appears toward the close of the work: the battle between the "snout of the anteater" and the "mouth of the other animal."[4] Out of these relationships the poems develop a complex series of metaphors and various rhetorical figures. The dialectic of elided desire in *Concealed Adventures* is expressed variously and from unique angles in each poem, exploring by this method the limitless possibilities of sexuality, which in turn are the equivalent of the endless strategies of the poetic act. Apart from the Oedipal situation in the poem "Call of the Desirous Man," one can find many other equally interesting instances of elided desire in this intriguing collection of poetry. In the poem "The Wife in the Scales" ("La esposa en la balanza"), the relationship between a husband and a wife is described as a desire of the "other": "That eagerness ... to pursue the other's morsel."†[5]

As a text, "Encounter with the False Man" ("Encuentro con el falso") is a more complicated poem than "Call of the Desirous Man" and "The Wife in the Scales" in that the use of rhetorical figures and the twists and changes of the various codes and references make it extremely difficult to follow any semblance of plot or anecdote. Still, this poem clearly is profoundly erotic: a man seduces a woman by reiterating that he is her son ("I am your son"), only to confess later the falsity of this Oedipal declaration: "I am not, but I say that I am your son."[6] This implicit declaration lends itself to various interpretations (as is characteristic of all of Lezama's poems), among others a rechanneling of "normalized"

---

* "el mar quiere decirnos ¿cenará conmigo esta noche?"
† "Ese afán ... de seguir el hilo del bocado ajeno."

desire. As Lacan has indicated, the erotic, in its phase succeeding the "normalization" of the Oedipal formation, must erase this bond that carries the man toward the woman by way of submerged feelings toward the mother, feelings that are prohibited by the laws against incest.[7] This is the memory repressed (elided) by consciousness, and from this comes the profound rupture implied in the declaration "I am your son." The poem "The Oval Portrait" ("El retrato ovalado") also concerns the same Oedipal theme, the eroticism of the wife as mother: "He fled, but after the scales, the wife hides herself as mother," "the desirous one who fled pays, seeing in the wife the oval mother."[*][8]

The multiplicity of codes in *Concealed Adventures* and the tensions between the various textual and anecdotal oppositions carry essentially the same point: poetry is a penetration of the nonrational realm, of the universal rhythm of desire that generates all the possibilities of creation. This investigation of the occult is here established as analogous to the sexual act and especially to the exceptional sexual eroticism of prohibited desire in which the woman is seen as a mother for whom her son hungers incestuously. Much of the basic symbology of the work is suggested in "The Watchman Begins His Circular Struggle" ("El guardián inicia el combate circular"), the last poem of *Concealed Adventures*, which carries desire to mythical dimensions and where the sexual act is expressed metaphorically in several ways.[9] In addition, the sexual poetics of *Concealed Adventures* marks the beginning of the possibility of creating a story, and thus these may be seen as the first poems in which Lezama starts to explore the novelization of poetry, a profound fictionalization that culminates in his *Paradiso* and *Oppiano Licario*. A study of these novels will uncover the development of many of the same themes and concerns addressed in his poetry.

One can begin to examine Lezama's *Paradiso* by noting that its central theme is the fictionalization of a pseudo-autobiographical poet's life, a man named José Cemí.[10] The perspective requires, moreover, that we investigate the meaning of the nexus between the vocation of poet and elements of "autobiographical" narrative. What meaning and importance can the poet's calling present when the protagonist of the narrative is "autobiographical," as is

---

[*] "Huyó, pero después de la balanza, la esposa se esconde como madre," "el deseoso que huyó paga viendo en la esposa la madre ovalada."

José Cemí? The possible responses to this question lead to a consideration of the bond between poetry and the conceptions of the subject and self-representation. Furthermore, this subject, who pretends to represent himself, is already fragmented by crisis because of alienation and seeks to rectify the separation that exists between himself and the world and between himself and language. The remainder of this chapter considers how such a search for poetic salvation is made in *Paradiso*.

Paradiso is a Lezamian contribution to the textual strategies of self-referential narrative. This novel positions itself both within and against the trajectory of autobiographical narratives beginning with the *Confessions* of St. Augustine. In almost all such works, despite the varied and at times opposing ideologies, the attempt is to give expression to the fragmentation of the subject and its relationship to its literary self-representation. The genealogy of this subgenre explores diverse strategies within the context of epistemological changes regarding conceptions of the subject.[11] Lezama's contribution to self-referential narrative is an answer to the romantic subversion of the medieval attitude toward the subject and its representation. How can an author be the subject of his or her own narration? How can the medium of language represent another medium, that of being? What is the meaning of the search for unity in a narration that is termed "autobiographical"? These are but a few of the questions that must be considered if we are to place Lezama's *Paradiso* in the trajectory of the self-referential novel.

The first seven chapters of *Paradiso* deal with the family history and the intellectual and sexual formation of José Cemí, who appears throughout this entire section of the novel as an extremely passive character. From the perspective of an omniscient third-person narrator, these first few chapters develop a complex series of relationships between ancestors, relatives, immediate family, and the friends of Cemí. Chapters 8 and 9 narrate the beginning of José Cemí's participation in the world of both friendship and history. These nine initial chapters are, without doubt, the closest to traditionally autobiographical narration. Nevertheless, all the events, episodes, and characters are intentionally fictionalized and transformed within the work into significant parts of Lezama's poetic system of the world.

Paradiso starts with the illness of José Cemí. His parents are out for the evening, and the child, in the middle of the night, is overcome with one of his frequent asthma attacks. It is worth noting that the protagonist, José Cemí, suffers from the same asthmatic condition as Lezama. In addition, asthma is an illness that interrupts natural respiratory functions, just as this novel is characterized from its beginning by a deliberate ailment that seeks a steady cadence, one that might substitute for the lack of natural rhythm.[12] It is also important to point out that the asthma attack occurs at night, when the parents are nowhere around. Several of the significant actions of the novel take place in the middle of the night, since darkness is a suitable context for an invitation to the unknown. The effect of these incidents is to situate us within the coordinates of Lezama's poetic system.

If *Paradiso* stands as a contribution to the self-referential novel, the contribution must be understood in terms of its experimental questionings and open challenges and not in terms of any particular adherence to the subgenre. It is true, however, that from the *Confessions* of St. Augustine up to the present there exists a trajectory of narratives that search for a kind of reparation of the self-representing subject. In his *Confessions*, Augustine concerns himself with his complete healing by writing out in full the history of his conversion. Here is an instance that presumes to transform the fragmentary nature of its subject through language. To evoke the past through language is to seek a present remedy. Thus, for Augustine, to write is to seek salvation by means of a self-analytical writing that will lift the narrating subject from his divided state and into a unity with God. From this standpoint, Augustine implies that he has access to the Transcendental Word, and that his soul can achieve a unified, spiritual creation at one with God.[13]

Augustine's theological view was continually challenged until, during the romantic period, a rupture developed that secularized the nature of the subject. Thus Wordsworth, in his *Prelude*, despite his awareness of Augustine's ideas, seeks the self-transformation and the mental growth of an *individual* subject centered primarily on the actual process of composing the poem. This romantic attitude emphasizes the paradoxes of the autobiographical caught in an era in which the role of the subject as a construct of the moral powers of mankind is being redefined.[14] Lezama, however, has surpassed the romantic conception of the subject as individual, and his protagonist's retrospection is carried out as a fiction that constitutes a new reality through the creative power of the Image. The attempt is to reconstruct the subject, language, and history by means of a poetic process that manifests itself through a metaphorical subject, specifically metaphorical since its function is to absorb all differences.

As we continue to explore the narrative development of *Paradiso*, we notice that the second chapter treats various events within Cemí's family in Cuba during the years 1910–17. Several episodes concern the ten-year-old Cemí at school. Also mentioned is a character called Mamita, the grandmother of three protégés of Colonel José Eugenio Cemí, the father of the novel's protagonist. From what we know about Lezama's family, there did exist a person called Mamita, a protégé of sorts of Lezama's father, but her actions in the novel are not the same as any facts we know about her.[15] For example, the novel relates that Mamita "moved between the dream world and the everyday world without establishing any difference,"* an indication of some mysterious element that erases the limits between visible reality and the *suprareal.* The chapter closes with a description of the Colonel dreaming. From the beginning of the work it has been emphasized that the Colonel is the force that gives unity to the universe of the novel; thus it seemed "his destiny was to fertilize a happy unity and prolong the instant that is given us in order to contemplate the wonders of integration and of harmony."†

The next chapter jumps back in time—to 1894. We are taken from Havana to Jacksonville and to the residence of the Olaya, the maternal family of José Cemí. In the universe of the novel, the contrast between the Olayas and the Cemís "mirrors" that of their biographical counterparts, the Lima and Lezama families, respectively.[16]

It is worth noting that an explicit theme of this chapter deals with the differences between Protestant theology and Catholicism. The polarities are established by the conversations of two characters: Florita, who represents Calvinist theology and favors free will against predestination, and Augusta (mother of Rialta),

---

* "Saltaba del sueño a lo cotidiano sin establecer diferencias" (p. 27).

† "Parecía que su destino era fecundar la alegre unidad y prolongar el instante en que nos es dado contemplar las ruedas de la integración y de la armonía" (p. 36).

who, from a Catholic perspective, cautions Florita against trusting too much in free will. According to Augusta (grandmother of the protagonist), human will is also mysterious: "when it is impossible to envision its ends is precisely when, for us, it becomes creative and poetic."* And so Lezama begins to discuss the relationship between destiny and the will, and it is clear—all the more so by what we know of the remainder of the novel and the body of Lezama's work—that Augusta's position is much nearer to that of the author of *Paradiso* than is Florita's. This idea of a mysterious will, which Lezama presents, is distinct not only from the Calvinist view but also from that of Nietzsche. The discussions between Augusta and Florita (presented in the novel as people without too much formal education) underline a typical technique of the novel: the characters often speak as if they were theologians or philosophers, even when they do not have any training of this kind, thus denying any semblance of realistic characterization.

This chapter also mentions the old woman Cambita, the mother of Augusta, said to be the daughter of a Puerto Rican official. This is a reference to the most distant branch of the family tree. Beyond this point nothing more is known of the Olaya line. Here memory fails and imagination is born; history ends and poetry begins. As has been mentioned, the Image sustains itself from the universe beyond the farthest limits and, precisely because it is unknown, is a continual invitation to the exercise of the imagination.

The fourth chapter takes place primarily in Cuba and relates some details about José Eugenio Cemí, the future father of the novel's protagonist. José Eugenio and his sisters have been living on income derived from a small business selling palm honey, which, in the novel, is a cure for asthmatics. This is yet another indication that the father of José Cemí appears as one who is called to remedy a flaw, in this case the asthma of his own son. The defects of respiration can be cured by palm honey, but, the novel states, the sick child must first lose his fear of darkness before the remedy can take effect. José Cemí must immerse himself in the world of Image and poetry to obtain a cure for his lack of natural breathing rhythm. The text also mentions that the

---

* "cuando ya no vemos sus fines es cuando se hace para nosotros creadora y poética." (pp. 46–47).

Olaya family returned from Jacksonville to Havana in 1902, the same year the Cuban Republic began. Thus the novel relates, in a fictional manner, not only to a self-referential narrative of the author but also to Cuban history.

Perhaps the most important event in the fifth chapter occurs when Alberto (brother of Rialta, the future mother of the protagonist) and José Eugenio attend a dance where they find Rialta. There José Eugenio and Rialta begin their romance. Also present at the dance is Tomás Estrada Palma (first president of Republican Cuba after the U.S. intervention, which lasted from 1898 to 1902). The events of the dance point to the novel's intention of integrating the political destiny of the country with the life of the protagonist.

Chapter 6 can be viewed as the beginning of the convergences that bring about Cemí's vocation as poet: the death of Colonel José Eugenio Cemí is narrated, and the vacuum that must be filled by poetry is defined. It is also mentioned that Mela, mother of don Andrés Olaya, suffers from memory loss, and thereby the situations of the two great-grandmothers of the protagonist (Mela and Cambita) represent a limit between memory and the imagination. Moreover, some of the events narrated at the beginning of this chapter are related to a fictionalized version of Cuba's War of Independence (1895–98). For example, the text describes the inspection of Mela's house by a number of Spaniards, thus connecting Cemí's great-grandmother with the struggle for national independence.

Furthermore, this chapter establishes a mythical relationship between Mela and Cemí, since both are asthmatic. Following this recollection of past events, the narration moves to a more recent period, the marriage of José Eugenio and Rialta, around 1910. Later, we read of José Eugenio trying to teach his five-year-old son, José Cemí, to swim. José Cemí is perilously close to drowning, and the father has to extend a finger to his son to save him. Both the son's inability to swim and the asthma cause the father to be ashamed of his son. Everything suggests that this section of the novel is given over to the efforts of the father to train his son within the rules of a masculine society, but the child seems unable to respond successfully to what is being taught. José Cemí also fails to understand the meaning of a story his father tells about the engravings of a *bachiller* (holder of a degree) and an *amolador* (knife-sharpener). While telling the story, the father erroneously says the word *bachiller* when he points to the *amolador*, and Cemí confuses the engravings every time he refers to them. Thus we are presented with a protagonist who falls short on three accounts: he lacks the natural rhythm of breathing because of his asthma, he cannot adopt the masculine rules of his father since he is unable to swim, and he mistakes the intended meaning of the story of the *bachiller* and the *amolador*. What is dealt with here, without any doubt, is a confusion of roles and a path contrary to accepted social behavior. These are the characteristics that signal the necessity to create a poetic universe that subverts the conventional rules and hurls itself against accepted limits.

Cemí's frequent nightmares, also described in this chapter, are particularly relevant at this juncture of the novel, since they are an early indication of his tendency to find a substitution for the reality that surrounds him. The clearest instance of this appears after the episode of the Colonel fighting against bandits in the city of Cruces. The protagonist has a nightmare in which he appears as a "general of invisible troops," thus indicating his poetic vocation that will eventually lead him to the creation of a new reality. In fact, the themes of *absence* and *image* are central to this chapter. Nevertheless, Cemí cannot yet "make analogies from the dissimilar." For the time being, the indications of his future vocation appear only as prophecy, in gestation, which manifests itself in the form of dreams. The child Cemí is thus pictured as filled with fright and terror.

The same chapter recounts how the Colonel has to move with his family to Pensacola, Florida, in order to participate in training with United States troops during World War I. The section is narrated with frequent allusions to the beginning of Cemí's destiny as poet of the Image of absence, "as if the reverse of those hours, which sound in other regions, had the true content of reality"*

One cold December night in Pensacola the family goes to see a motion picture, and the Colonel does not wear his overcoat. There has been a flu epidemic, and he comes down with a cold. The Colonel is hospitalized, and this is the last time they see him

---

* "como si el reverso de aquellas horas, que suena en otras regiones, fuera el que tuviese contenido" (p. 157).

alive. The death of the Colonel is described in the novel as something that left "a truncated and indecipherable destiny." The Colonel died at thirty-three years of age, the same as José Lezama Lima's father. José Cemí is able to tolerate his desolation upon seeing his father dead in the hospital only because of a stranger's fixed gaze. This mysterious character, named Oppiano Licario, had been a friend of the Colonel for a long while and had promised him to sustain José Cemí. As part of his insistence that poetry situates itself in the vacuum left by the absence of nature, Lezama presents Oppiano Licario as a character with no psychological or fictional justification.[17] What is being dealt with here is not reality in the sense intended by the positivists, but a kind of suprareality, a reality fictionalized by the poetic Image. Within this formative process of the poet of the Image, the Colonel, right before his death, had said his purpose was to die and the purpose of Rialta was "to be witness to my death." At this stage, José Cemí's destiny remains in the hands of his mother on one side and Oppiano Licario on the other.

We can view the Colonel as emblematic of the Father, of Nature, and his absence points to the flaw within the natural order that would permit unity within the subject. Now Cemí has been orphaned and must find some replacement for the presence of his natural father. The substitute is Oppiano Licario, whose role in the novel is to serve as an intermediary between the absence of the father and the poetic vocation of Cemí. If asthma deprives Cemí of a natural respiratory rhythm, the death of the Colonel removes from him a natural father's presence. Yet with the support of Oppiano Licario (at the moment of the Colonel's death and later on, at the end of the novel), there is the aspiration to fill, if vicariously, the lack of natural order with the creative power of poetry. This aspiration appears in the novel as the drive to achieve what Lezama names "ritmo hesicástico" (loosely translated as "perfect rhythm").[18] In Lezama's poetic system, this rhythm, founded on the absence of nature, voices a limitless creativity, which is an incentive to pursue a state of salvation. Thus Cemí's vocation is to be the poet whose creativity is a response to the absence of the natural.

The following chapter takes place for the most part in Augusta's house. The widow and her children begin to adjust to the loss of the Colonel. In one instance, Rialta is playing jacks with her children when, across the flagstones, there appears the figure of the Colonel in his military clothes with "the face of the absent father." It is an indication of the overlapping area between the fragmentary and totality, of an equation between the part and the whole. This is the image of the father that announces the destiny of the child. After this episode, a series of family events is related; in each case, there appears something that hints at the destiny of José Cemí. One of the most commented-upon episodes of the chapter involves the death of Alberto, maternal uncle of Cemí. This passing reaffirms the absence of a paternal figure in Cemí's life, yet in this poetic system it is precisely this vacuum that permits generation of the Image that, in turn, is able to bring together the dispersed fragments of visible reality.

The second part of the novel (chapters 7–14) is progressively fictionalized and less "autobiographical," especially from chapter 9 on. Throughout this last section, with perhaps the exception of the student demonstrations of chapter 9, it is difficult to determine what is related to Lezama's life and what is solely fiction. The distinctions are particularly blurred in the eighth chapter where the novel deals basically with instances of homosexual activities.[19] It is indisputable, however, that the eighth chapter of *Paradiso* presents several of the most explicit homosexual scenes ever narrated in Spanish literature. Chapters 9 and 10 also contain dialogues of great profundity regarding the various interpretations of homosexuality in world history.

The eighth chapter deals mainly with events related to Cemí at school, where he makes a series of sexual discoveries. Here is described the prodigious sexuality of Farraluque and Leregas. The overwhelming sexuality of this chapter is important for two reasons: because it appears soon after the deaths of Cemí's uncle and father and because it is almost always homosexual.[20] Once the father and uncle are gone, the boy has to "invent" a sexual code. This emphasizes the objective of the novel: in the face of the absence of a natural order, it is necessary to seek a substitute in the *supranatural*, liberated from time and reproduction.[21] Within this context, the homosexuality in *Paradiso* becomes an emblem of poetry: it is a search for the similar without the necessity of concerning oneself with time and reproduction. Instead of attempting to make an exact replica, it aspires to a creativity that goes beyond the "natural" toward a state that Lezama defines as *hipertélico* (beyond the limits). Homosexuality is then a metaphor that is inscribed into the center of the vacuum created by the absence of a natural order. Within the universe of the novel, it is perceived by several characters (especially those who represent established values) as an unaccepted or "unnatural" behavior. Homosexuality in *Paradiso* is also presented as an excess that, precisely because it goes beyond the permitted limits, announces the possibility of a creative surplus that Blake calls "the palace of wisdom achieved by the road of excess." It is in this sense that the erotic and the aesthetic in Lezama find their greatest creative potential, suggesting that only what goes beyond the limits can lead to a penetration of the new and the unknown.

The last section of chapter 9 is given over almost completely to the theme of homosexuality. We find Cemí at the university with his friends Fronesis and Foción, the three conversing extensively about the possible meaning of homosexuality. Fronesis propounds a series of opinions on homosexuality, which Foción sees as a psychoanalytic interpretation of the theme. For Fronesis, all sexual deviation is a manifestation of ancestral memory, but he considers sex, like poetry, "convincing stuff, not problematical" (p. 263). Fronesis comes close to a Freudian viewpoint when he notes, "The seasons of a man's life do not necessarily have to fall in succession; there are men in whom the state of innocence, this living in a state of childhood, perseveres all life long." This opinion approaches the Freudian idea that sexual "deviation" results from a fixation at some stage of childhood. Fronesis says, "The child ... fixated forever in childhood, always has a tendency toward similar sexuality, that is, to seek in sexuality an 'other,' yet an 'other' similar to himself." This is why the primitive, the child, and the poet have profound similarities; they sustain the latent mythical time of transformation, "which is the instant in which one can return to inhabit this state of innocence."*

Foción argues that Fronesis's psychoanalytic interpretation attempts to explain the inexplicable and suffers from a "mechanicism" and "causalism" that cannot be justified. For Foción— whose role in the novel is homosexual— homosexuality is not a

---

* "El niño ... que se fija para siempre en la niñez, tiene siempre tendencia a la sexualidad semejante, es decir, a situar en el sexo la otredad, el otro semejante a sí mismo"; "que es el momento en que se puede volver a habitar ese estado de inocencia" (p. 264).

deviation, a vice, or a voluntary decision; it is something more profound than any justification. Here Foción voices a series of ideas that move away from a dialogue about homosexuality and into a conception of poetry similar to Lezama's. Foción says "all which is seeded, as the Taoists say, is seeded in empty space. And all that is sown ... is given unto voiceless space that at the end takes voice."*

One of the most dramatic passages during Foción's exposition about homosexuality is when he paraphrases Ecclesiastes ("There is the straight way, which has an end and the end is death"), then continues propounding the search for the "other way." In this manner, the text reaffirms the idea of homosexuality as a search for the *supranatural*, liberated from the constraints of reproduction and time. Foción's conclusion about sexual "deviation" is as follows: "All that seems deviant to us today comes from a form of reminiscence or from something I will presume to call a *hipertelia* [that which goes beyond every limit] of immortality."† This is followed by a series of commentaries on the varied attitudes of some of the most renowned homosexuals in history: the two Barba Jacob's (one from the sixteenth century and the Colombian from the twentieth century who took the previous Jacob's name), Leonardo da Vinci, Julius Caesar, Cesar Borgia, Oscar Wilde, and so on. Also mentioned are recent texts (recent for the period in which Lezama was writing *Paradiso*); among them the work of sexologist Havelock Ellis, which indicated that 75 percent of English males had experimented with homosexuality (p. 270).

After this conversation, Foción and Cemí speak of Platonic dialogues, surmising that these have always served as the models for this type of inquiry.[22] Cemí begins to elaborate upon a set of theories regarding essence and being and then moves into a treatment of love, sex, and desire. What Cemí wishes to explore here is whether sexual desire arises from a memory of a perfect state of unity and being or from the desire to form a new species or a new

---

* "Toda siembra profunda, como decían los taoístas, es en el espacio vacío. Y toda siembra que nos hace temblar ... se hace en el espacio sin respuesta, que al fin da una respuesta" (pp. 265–66).

† "Todo lo que hoy nos parece desvío sexual, surge en una reminiscencia, o en algo que yo me atrevería a llamar, sin temor a ninguna pedantería, una hipertelia de la inmortalidad" (p. 268).

reality. As a way of creating a context for the discussion, he mentions a number of classical references but prefers to discuss (though often with a high degree of unorthodox interpretation) the Catholic theologians, particularly Augustine and Thomas Aquinas. Cemí and Foción talk about the different interpretations of homosexuality found in these two authors. Cemí is surprised to find that Augustine is far more violently opposed to homosexual activity than is Aquinas. Both theologians agree that homosexual activity is a "vice against nature," but each defines "nature" in a different way. Cemí finds it astonishing that someone like Augustine, who had read deeply in Plato and had experienced intense male friendship in his youth, would be more against homosexuality than Aquinas, who was considered celibate all his life. Cemí can only conclude that these differences of opinion arise from Aquinas's respect for the body as God's creation (p. 286).

To give historical perspective to Cemí's comments, it is helpful to consider John Boswell's 1980 publication studies on the varying social attitudes toward homosexuality in the Middle Ages.[23] He reminds us that Augustine (354–430) came from rural North Africa (to which he eventually returned) and wrote his "confessions" as a response to the enormous impact that he experienced as a consequence of urban life. According to Boswell, Augustine's "furious" repentance can be seen as a return to rural values. However, despite growing moral intolerance from the third century on, hostility against homosexuality, notes Boswell, was in no way organized (neither at the legal nor at the theological level), as it was in the High Middle Ages of the thirteenth and fourteenth centuries. This epoch, in which Aquinas published his *Summa*, was marked by profound social unrest, a possible cause of extremes in both governmental and ecclesiastical authoritarianism. Aquinas's *Summa* systematized not only religious ideas but also some of the most extreme prejudices of the time. This ideological codification served as the base for many of the religious and social repressions of modern Western Europe and its colonies, according to Boswell.

After detailed descriptions in chapter 8 of sexual activities at school, the novel narrates a trip Cemí takes to Santa Clara with his grandmother and aunt. In Santa Clara, he meets Ricardo Fronesis, the son of a lawyer, who is described as strong and beautiful. It soon becomes apparent that Fronesis is going to play an important role in Cemí's vocation. Fronesis appears as the prototype of happiness, stoicism, dignity, and spiritual health, even though in the final chapters we discover progressively that his personality and family history are filled with complexity and contradiction.

The ninth chapter relates a very important experience in Cemí's development. We see Cemí actively integrating himself with national history by participating in a revolutionary student demonstration. In Lezama's life, a parallel situation occurred during the dictatorship of Gerardo Machado, in 1930. Cemí's involvement in extreme political activity represents a transformation in his life, since it is at this point that the protagonist begins to immerse himself into the reality of his poetry and of Cuban history. The student demonstration in *Paradiso* is the fictionalization of an actual event that was important not only in the life and imagination of Lezama but also in the history of Cuba. A protest against the dictatorship of Gerardo Machado that occurred on 30 September 1930 resulted in the death of the student leader Rafael Trejo. Lezama was an active participant and in an interview many years later—in fact, after the 1959 revolution—affirmed that "no higher honor do I prefer than my participation on that morning."[24] In one of his lesser-known pieces, titled simply "Reading" ("Lectura"), Lezama fictionalized the historical event in which Trejo died. In one sense, the pertinent section of "Reading" is a reelaboration of the passage of *Paradiso* previously discussed.[25] In Lezama's poetical history the blood of Trejo flows down the steps of the University of Havana and later reappears, in a positive manner, in the Sierra Maestra. What Lezama attempts here is to include the death of Trejo with the totality of his poetic system and particularly within his vision of the history of Cuba and Latin America.[26] The historical "fact" is converted into a symbol within a text, which the poet, through the metaphoric process, recovers and rewrites in another text. This approach attempts to view history as integrated into a compact, dynamic fictional network, rather than as a dissemination of scattered fragments. Its goal is to diminish the distance between a historical fact and poetic imagination and writing. The death of Trejo is only one of the many examples indicating how Lezama incorporates accepted historical events within the context of a fictionalized history.

Other important events in this section of the novel include the beginning of the friendship among Cemí, Fronesis, and Foción; the conversation between Cemí and his mother; and Cemí's reading of the *Wilhelm Meister*. During the violence of the student demonstration, Cemí feels the absence of his father's hand but is rescued from the confusion and gunshots by Fronesis. Since Eugenio Foción was with Fronesis at the time, this marks the beginning of the strong friendship between the three characters. From this moment in the novel, Fronesis and Foción appear as options open to the subject in crisis who seeks his vocation and personal destiny. Once Cemí escapes the tumult he returns to his house and more important to his mother, Rialta. The danger from which her son has just escaped causes Rialta to realize that Cemí is starting to take his father's place. She advises her son always to seek the most difficult path, thus helping him at this crucial moment to achieve his destiny as poet of the "extralimitation." It is also significant that the night after the student revolt, Cemí responds to his new situation by reading Goethe's *Wilhelm Meister*, an act that suggests a relationship between the *Bildungsroman* and *Paradiso*. In fact Lezama said in an interview that *Paradiso* is "a Cuban *Wilhelm Meister*."[27]

The beginning of the tenth chapter offers Cemí's thoughts on the conversation with Fronesis and Foción. We read that he is "also giving thought to the novel hidden behind those words." This suggests that the very novel we are reading is beginning to take shape in the protagonist's mind.

The remainder of chapter 10 is devoted to an exploration of the past and present of Fronesis and Foción, as well as to a number of long discussions on Hegel and Nietzsche. What is being suggested here by the juxtaposition of Fronesis and Foción on the one hand and Hegel and Nietzsche on the other? There are sufficient clues within the text to indicate that Fronesis and Foción are to be read not only as alter egos of the complex Cemí-Lezama personality, but also as symbolic representations of the development of Lezama's thought. This particular instance seems to indicate that Lezama, through the characters of Fronesis and Foción, assimilates the ideological extremes represented by Hegel and Nietzsche, respectively. This relationship implies an interesting hypothesis: that Fronesis appears as Lezama's interpretation of Hegelian philosophy, whereas Foción functions likewise in regard to Nietzschean thought.

From the moment of their first meeting, Cemí views Fronesis as a guide toward his true vocation, especially in the temporary absence of Oppiano Licario. For Cemí, Fronesis is the epitome of uniformity of character: strong, tender, friendly, and ceremonious; whereas Foción sees Fronesis as the product of an enigmatic past. Foción points out that Fronesis was raised by his aunt because his real mother never loved Fronesis's father. This relationship serves to emphasize the "bad" natural mother and the "good" step-mother. Moreover, Fronesis, though appearing very masculine and without complexes, has a difficult time sustaining satisfactory sexual relations with his girlfriend, Lucía. The center of his problem is "his memory of another dancer" (his mother was a dancer), creating a situation too obviously Oedipal to be ignored. Yet since Fronesis never knew his mother, the association must be taken within a mythical context. Additionally, this emphasis on the Oedipal is closely related to his psychoanalytic opinions on homosexuality.

Cemí considers Fronesis's method of knowing as profoundly critical: "He learns, then pulverizes what he has learned with equal, critical dignity." Of Foción, Cemí feels "there had been a root error, his conduct never acquired form ... but always remained at the stage of a striving potential."* Cemí's opinions of his two friends seem to signal, in the case of Fronesis, the critical-dialectical methodology of Hegel and, in the case of Foción, Lezama's rejection of Nietzsche. For the author of *Paradiso*, Nietzsche's radical transformation of values never arrives at a creative form, never achieves the assimilative power of the Image.

Cemí, in a typical philosophical discussion with his friend Fronesis, says that there exist two Nietzsches, the one who reacts against academia and the one who presumes to place himself "beyond the law." This "extralimitation" seems to suggest a creative dimension, but, according to Lezama, Nietzsche does not quite manage to exploit this possibility. The author of *Zarathustra* "did not inhabit the island"; he constructed nothing within the vacuum left by his deliberate subversion of all established values (p. 322). For Cemí, Fronesis "knows what he lacks and searches for it assiduously," whereas Nietzschean criticism

---

* "había en su raíz un equívoco, su conducta no adquiría nunca forma, una forma última del devenir de la materia, según la frase de los escolásticos, sino una potencialidad deseosa" (p. 298).

(equated here with Foción) does not know what it seeks, destroying all that it does know without constructing anything in its place. Thus with Fronesis, contrary to Foción, "fate plays itself out in a continuum." Finally, it is Foción who establishes the direct relationship between Fronesis and Hegel when he says to Cemí: "If you don't know his blood, you can't discern the spiritual possibility in Fronesis ... he is the horse who is ridden by the absolute spirit, recalling Hegel's expression."*

It is important for the characterization of Cemí's friends to establish not only that Fronesis has two mothers but also that Foción has two fathers. Both the adopted father of Foción and the adopted mother of Fronesis are, by far, superior to their "originals," indicating the possible perfection to be obtained by substituting the Image for the "natural." It is clearly stated within the novel that the work of the three friends lies in overcoming the frustrations of familial destiny, especially, as we might expect, in the case of Cemí. This was Foción's environment: "surrounded by insanity, he grew with no knowledge of original sin. His feelings were not taught to segregate the sexual from the social but rather all was information that either advanced toward or retreated from the image."†

It is possible that Foción is presented here as an image of modern man guided by the scientific spirit ("the careful attention of reason in the service of insanity"). Or perhaps he represents Nietzschean thought, which, though antiscientific, examined the philosophical abyss minutely but without arriving at true creativity. Whatever the case, the description is of an empty, sterile madness that Lezama at times attributes as much to Nietzsche as to the scientific spirit. However, in spite of all these criticisms against certain aspects of Nietzschean thought, we will later see how Lezama, in his posthumous novel *Oppiano Licario*, projected a final solution for his poetic system that favors Foción over Fronesis.

Cemí says of Foción that he tries "to demonstrate naturally a

---

* "Si no conoces su sangre, no podrás conocer la posibilidad del espíritu en Fronesis ... es el caballo que monta el espíritu absoluto, recordando la expresión de Hegel" (pp. 300–301).

† "rodeado por la locura creció sin pecado original. Sus sentidos no segregaban materia concupiscible, sino datos de conocimiento que avanzaban o retrocedían hasta la imagen" (pp. 338–39).

nature not at all natural."* Although he is open about his homosexuality, Foción was married and has a child. It is also significant that Foción is associated here with a statue of Narcissus, which the text describes as "the image of the image, of nothingness." Furthermore, he amplifies this observation with a thought of Lao-Tze: "the egg hatches in the vacuum." This combining of the image of Narcissus and the thought of Lao-Tze suggests the Lezamian idea of mythical creation whereby a form of creation rises from the absence of natural order while rejecting a narcissistic self-contemplation devoid of any productive creativity.

Later in the same chapter, Cemí looks for Fronesis at the university and finds him discussing Nietzsche. The key phrase in his discourse is "the transmutation of all values." According to Fronesis, the principal values Nietzsche chooses to subvert are: (a) "objectivity" (in the Hegelian sense); (b) "compassion in the face of suffering" (in an essentially Christian form); (c) "the sense of history" (referring to all historiography prior to Nietzsche, including Hegel's); (d) "the giving over to foreign taste" (in the context of a Wagnerian nationalism that Nietzsche was to later forego or at least modify); (e) "the vulgarity of common details" (this relates, in one respect, to the modern democratic spirit); and (f) "the scientific spirit," which both Nietzsche and Lezama reject (pp. 321-25). Fronesis says of Nietzsche that in his obsession to subvert everything, he reacts against many values that certainly need revaluation, but also rejects others better left alone. Fronesis voices Lezama's idea that Nietzsche's greatest error was his all-out confrontation with the religious spirit.

Cemí agrees with Fronesis about Nietzsche, but in his own discussion prefers to explore in even more detail the points raised by his friend, complimenting Fronesis on having opinions that are true to his name: the wise, the flowing, the mover, the opposite of "the frantic search for the new." This idea stated by Cemí is in keeping with many of Lezama's ideas. On the one hand, Lezama criticizes Nietzsche's interpretation of classical Greek antiquity, in which the author of The Birth of Tragedy explores the absence of Dionysian creativity in Greek sensibility. On the other hand, Lezama insists that Nietzsche's greatest error lies in attempting to subvert all Christian values. Lezama feels that by doing so, many

---

* "mostrar naturalmente una naturaleza poco natural" (p. 332).

significant and creative values within the Hellenic (especially Orphism and the Pythagorean) and Christian tradition are also lost (p. 322).

Cemí comments that Nietzsche, in *Zarathustra*, seems "hungry despite his satisfaction," but adds that "he never demonstrates ... creative hunger, which goes beyond limits in search of the complementary, untarnished, and the mysterious."* Cemí also establishes a relationship between Nietzsche and Hegel by saying: "His [Nietzsche's] reaction against the spirit of objectivity was one of the manifestations of his hatred of Hegel, especially when Hegel would presume to carry the identity principle of the Greeks to its logical end and derive from this the spirit of objectivity and the absolute." And Cemí adds: "Nietzsche was a man of rare critical intensity as demonstrated by his challenging the spirit of objectivity in his time, but also a man of little depth when he failed to realize that the absence of the spirit of objectivity demonstrates the presence of the Holy Spirit."† At this point in the conversation Fronesis intervenes, attacking Nietzsche for his anti-Christian attitude toward those who suffer. This, says Fronesis, shows Nietzsche's ignorance about both the Greek and medieval cultures, as clearly evidenced by his erroneous supposition that all positive values originated in the Renaissance.

Contrary to his earlier attacks, Cemí's comments on Nietzsche's *Ecce Homo* support several Nietzschean postulates, specifically those that refer to the subversion of the "historical sense" and the "scientific spirit." In regard to the historical, however, Nietzsche's views are only partially supported by Cemí. For him, the true value of Nietzsche's thought lies in its attack on the "scientific spirit," which Cemí considers to be "belittling" (p. 327). It is through these opinions that Lezama indicates both the limits and the possibilities offered by Nietzsche and incorporated

---

* En el mismo Zaratustra, nos dice que tiene hambre dentro de su saciedad, pero nunca tiene hambre hipertélica, creadora, que va más allá de su finalidad, para buscar complementarios inocentes y misteriosos" (p. 322).

† "Su reacción contra el espíritu objetivo, era una de las manifestaciones de su odio a Hegel, cuando éste quiso llevar el principio de identidad de los griegos a sus últimas consecuencias, derivando el espíritu objetivo, absoluto.... Nietzsche fue un hombre de una rara intensidad crítica cuando en su época reaccionó contra el espíritu objetivo, pero de escasa profundidad cuando no pudo captar que no hay espíritu objetivo porque hay Espíritu Santo" (pp. 322–23).

into the Lezamian poetic system of the world. Nietzsche's most valuable contribution is his antiscientific spirit and his attack against positivistic historicism. But from Lezama's point of view, this must be interpreted carefully and, for that matter, only partially accepted. What Lezama assimilates from Nietzsche is the conception of history as something constructed metaphorically, like a narrative or fiction. There is not an absence of historical conception in Lezama, but rather a tendency toward what we may call "idealist providentialism," a sense of history as an ideal progression toward a *supranatural* betterment.

Lezama's "idealism" differs markedly from Hegel's. Instead of postulating the progress of the Idea toward a greater self-awareness, Lezama's idealism deals with the progress toward the universal mystery of poetry, toward the concealed rhythm of the Image. Lezama's "providentialism" has come to signify that *supranatural* element that permeates his entire poetic system, and that brings him to reject Hegel's opinion of a work of art as the product of an "arbitrary will." This, says Cemí, is equivalent to "affirming that the artist is the counselor of his own god."* It is precisely at this juncture that Lezama connects Hegel with Mallarmé: "At the end of *Introduction to Absolute Knowledge*, Hegel closes with a line that could have been a delight for the master Stephen: 'From the cup of this reign of the spirits flows its own infinity.' But for Hegel, the reign of the spirits is self-awareness, an awareness of identity. When he broke the relationship between the creator and the created by an excess of pride, he distanced himself from all true creation."† Cemí points out that Mallarmé "derived pure poetry from the absolute spirit of Hegel. He read Hegel's work on the absolute spirit with great passion."‡

These and other commentaries lead to an inevitable conclu-

---

* "afirmar que el artista es el consejero de su dios" (pp. 322–23).

† "Al final de su *Introducción al saber absoluto*, Hegel termina con un versículo que hubiera hecho las delicias del maestro Estéfano: 'De la copa de este reino de los espíritus espuma para sí su infinitud', sólo que en Hegel el reino de los espíritus es el espíritu que se sabe a sí mismo como espíritu, es la conciencia de la identidad. Al romper la relación entre el creador y la criatura, por el orgullo que enfatiza la criatura, toda verdadera creación le fue ajena" (p. 323).

‡ "Mallarmé derivó la poesía pura del espíritu absoluto hegeliano. Era un apasionado lector de la obra hegeliana sobre el espíritu absoluto" (p. 322).

sion: at this point in the novel, Cemí is drawn by the perfection of Mallarmé's symbolist poetics. The question that arises here is: in what way and to what consequence is the poetics of Lezama related to that of Mallarmé? To answer this question, we will investigate the nexus between Lezama and Mallarmé regarding the subject divided in crisis and the separation between subject, world, and language.

Lezama devoted a number of essays to the exploration of Mallarmé's work and to the relationship of that work to his own. In "New Mallarmé II" ("Nuevo Mallarmé II"), Lezama offers the author of *Crise de Vers* the most effusive eulogies one might imagine, saying that he is "one of the great centers of poetic polarization situated at the beginning of contemporary poetry, who possesses one of the most powerful and enigmatic sensibilities that exist in the history of images." Lezama adds: "I think, at times, just as at the end of a Greek chorus or the appearance of a new epiphany, that his pages and the whispers of his resonances will one day be lifted up to be read by the gods."[*28]

The relationship between the poetics of Mallarmé and Lezama has already been studied in depth by Rubén Ríos-Ávila, but I wish to further explore this relationship. To this end, we might begin by insisting that the aesthetics of Mallarmé serves, among other things, as a crucial step in Lezama's process of assimilating and transcending the ideological extremes represented by Hegel and Nietzsche. Concerning *Paradiso* in particular, we have already established the hypothesis that Fronesis and Foción represent Lezama's fictionalizations of Hegelian and Nietzschean thought, respectively. At a key moment of his formation as poet, Cemí manages to transcend the artistic positions represented by his two friends precisely by assimilating the aesthetics of Mallarmé. This accomplishment also permits him to incorporate Oppiano Licario's poetics, which is strongly suggestive of Mallarmé's. Later in the narration of *Paradiso* (and even more so in the novel *Oppiano*

---

* "uno de los grandes centros de polarización poéticos, situado en el inicio de la poesía contemporánea y una de las actitudes más enigmáticas y poderosas que existen en la historia de las imágenes.... A veces pienso, como en el final de un coro griego o de una nueva epifanía, que sus páginas y el murmullo de sus timbres, serán algún día alzados ... para ser leído por los dioses."

Licario), Cemí forms his own poetic system, transcending both the poetics of Oppiano Licario and that of Mallarmé.

A poem, for Mallarmé, is an essential negation that is constructed as a totality in opposition to the Ideal, thus engendering a radical opposition between the creative desire and the poem. Mallarmé is therefore considered to be the prototype of a modern poet since in his aesthetics the creative act takes a fundamental negativity as its basis. The relationship that he establishes with his creative desire appears as a form of extreme resentment owing to the inability to overcome the fundamental lack that undermines every act of creation.[29] Clearly then, even though both Mallarmé and Lezama base their creations upon an absence, for the former this vacuum is the cause of a radical frustration, whereas for the latter it is cause for an overwhelming happiness. Lezama's vision of absence as the source of elation originates in the conception that such a void, precisely because it is the moment prior to the world of differentiation, is transformed into the creative incentive to inhabit the vacuum, to spill over into poetry.[30] This is closely related to the theme we have been exploring throughout chapter 9: that *Paradiso* and other Lezamian texts attempt to offer a metaphorical bridge in response to the invitation to creativity inherent in the absence of natural order, thus transforming this void into the creative source of all possibility. The Image of the Lezamian *supranature,* more than an unapproachable negativity, is a moment of innocence waiting to express itself to the visible world. This *supranature,* which comes to inhabit the vacuum, since it is the instant prior to all differentiation, also contains within it the potential to redeem the fragmentation of the subject in crisis and the separation between the subject, the world, and language.

Ríos-Ávila says that Lezama, like Mallarmé, is both Orphic and Hermetic in the sense that in both their poetics and their work, poetry is defined as an incursion into the deep regions of language where a lack of distinction exists between man and nature and, therefore, cannot be perceived by the conceptual method.[31] Nevertheless, Lezama and Mallarmé differ precisely in the meaning that each one gives to poetry and, for that matter, to the relationship between the subject, the world, and language. Mallarmé creates a formalized language that distances the poet from the object of his or her creative desire, whereas for Lezama this same discourse will not bring about a radical separation but a poetry that is totally embracing. Because of its assimilative power, Lezamian poetry is a bridge between the subject, the world, and language.[32]

Lezama does not renounce the Ideal, but rather transforms the Mallarmean "nausea of the material world" into a form of happiness.[33] In this context, the Mallarmean poet feels devoured by his or her own creation, a mere instrument at the mercy of an impersonal creative force devoid of any meaning. For Lezama, to the contrary, the poem is not a destruction of the subject as the creator but is rather a transformation of this subject into a redeemed metaphor, *redeemed* because it aspires to convert the vacuum left by an absence of natural order into a *supranature*. The distinctions between the subject who creates and the poem that has been created are erased, as well as the differences between the image of the created and the "exterior world." The Image, embracing the subject and language, dissolves both into a creative negation. Despite the lack of natural order (or perhaps precisely because there is such a lack), this absence possesses the magnetism that attracts what has not yet been created and brings it closer to the realization of creation. This force of the vacuum of the Image weaves a kind of redeemed *telos* oriented toward a total creativity. Thus the comparison of the Lezamian Image and the Mallarmean "absence" indicates that though the Image is in one sense also an "emptiness," it is not *only* "nothingness" but the source of a redeeming creativity, the negation of a negation.

Lezama's own views on this topic can be seen in chapter 11 of *Paradiso*: "Within him [i.e., Cemí] what was not, was; the invisible occupied center stage in the visible, converting itself into the visible through dizzying possibility; absence was presence, penetration, the *ocupatio* of the Stoics. Absence in him was never the reverse of Genesis, which had been the case with Mallarmé, but to the contrary was as natural as the bodies that were unfolding the marvels and proportions of rhythm."*

---

* "En él lo que no estaba, estaba; lo invisible ocupaba el primer plano en lo visible, convirtiéndose en un visible de una vertiginosa posibilidad; la ausencia era presencia, penetración, *ocupatio* de los estoicos. La ausencia no era nunca en él ese Génesis al revés, que se ha señalado en Mallarmé, por el contrario era tan naturaleza como los cuerpos desenvolviendo las proporciones del ritmo" (p. 349).

To elaborate the poetic system of *Paradiso*, we can examine the moment in chapter 11 when Fronesis delivers a poem dedicated to Cemí entitled "Portrait of Cemí" ("Retrato de Cemí"). The poem characterizes the protagonist of the novel as one whose "will can seek shapes in the shadow," (pp. 359–60), indicating that Fronesis is aware of Cemí's poetic vocation. After the story of the dedication of the poem, we are shown another aspect of the development of Lezamian vision. Cemí ponders the existence, within the same temporal unity, of events that are not only different but of contrary meanings. For example, while Fronesis is at the university speaking of his interpretation of St. George killing the two-headed dragon, Foción is in New York having sexual relations with a brother and a sister. Thus Lezama juxtaposes a commentary about a mythological figure destroying a monster with two contrary tendencies with the occurrence of sexual activity, also of contrary tendencies, with no apparent resolution. This juxtaposition serves as an introduction to the elaboration of the relationship between time, space, and poetic knowledge in *Paradiso*. Here Lezama explains "gnostic space" as inviting interpretation in order to give meaning to sensible elements. Gnostic space transforms quantity to "enchanted quantity" ("cantidad hechizada"), shaped by the metaphorical subject. This is a space without a preestablished natural order, precisely because of its dynamic lack, inviting the human subject to give meaning to it through a metaphorical process. All these meditations lead Cemí to realize that the transformation process has a temporal root, affirming that the Image, far from drawing itself from the essence of Being, or *logos*, is the substance of the unfolding of time. Cemí therefore realizes time itself is the reverse face of the Image.

Along with the topics of space and time, this chapter deals with the theme of reconciliation of contrary tendencies. The story is told of a heated argument between Foción and Dr. Fronesis (Fronesis's father), precipitated by the latter's discovery of Foción homosexuality and his feelings toward Fronesis. Later, when Fronesis learns of the encounter, there is a great family quarrel that results in reconciliation. This development is especially significant for María Teresa (Fronesis's stepmother), since it emblematically concerns a reconciliation with the stepmother, the symbolic substitute for nature in the subject's search for his destiny. Such a quest is specifically mentioned in chapter 11 in a passage describing the sickness and death of the grandmother Augusta. Before she dies, Augusta states her satisfaction in seeing Cemí already on the path of his poetic calling. Augusta tells him: "what is right for you is to capture the rhythm of growth." Coincidentally, Cemí discovers that Foción has been admitted to the psychiatric ward of the same hospital where Augusta is dying, although by the end of the chapter Foción has recovered. Foción's mental state will later prove to be an important element in *Oppiano Licario*'s poetic system.

Cemí's meditations about time continue in chapter 12. His investigations are presented through the narration of two dreams and a number of extraordinary events. With this section of the novel Lezama develops his account without losing sight of one of his main model-parodies: the *Paradiso* of Dante. The third part of the *Divine Comedy* explains that in order to achieve the vision of earthly paradise, the pilgrim must first experience a series of dreams that articulate a reality distinct from, if parallel to, the reality of the vigil. Thus in the *Paradiso* of Lezama, in order to arrive at the height of poetic understanding, the reader must also pass through dreams and fantastic stories that signal poetic reality beyond the realm of causality. Time is seen here as a submerged temporality that aspires to an undifferentiated moment, stemming from and moving toward the *supranatural* where there is no separation between subject, world, and language. This is another example of a fictionalized search for a universal rhythm serving as the source of creativity.

Continuing the elaboration of Lezama's vision of poetic rhythm, this chapter recounts the dream of a battle fought by a captain named Atrio Flaminio. Here Lezama seems to be interested in the contrast between what happens in the actual confrontation between the two armies and the celebration after the battle is over. The festivities are carried out by "defeated gymnasts" who, through their dance, search for a magic beat that will save them from their present condition and liberate them from the trap of successive time. Thus the dancers resemble poets in search of a hidden pulse beyond the limits of chronology. Nevertheless, Lezama's objective at this point is not to freeze time but to search for the fundamental, mysterious rhythm of the Image.

Another episode related to Lezama's concerns with temporality is the story of Juan Longo, an old music critic who puts himself in a deep sleep to conquer time. However, it is made clear that there is no attempt to bring "a subject to the dream, but, to the contrary, to prolong indefinitely what is already in the dream."* This is basically a subtle way to emphasize that the text is not proposing a kind of surrealism or oneirism, but attempting to achieve a sense of rhythm that extends beyond the dream itself. Finally, the story line questions the contemporary idea that considers all temporality and signification as an expression of the *in between* (p. 426). Lezama rejects this idea in the following way: "He [the sleeping musician] has conquered time as an *in between*, as conceived by a few contemporaries, since in his dream it is impossible to separate the past from that time that he is still elaborating. This *in between*, which seems to be the last refuge of dialectics among mortals, it is the negation of all penetration."† Once he has established the critique of the *in between*, Lezama proposes his concept of the rhythm of the Image that exists in order to give substance to the vacuum (pp. 425–26).

In chapter 13, Lezama lightens the extreme discursiveness and philosophical discussions in order to deliver a simpler anecdote, the story of an almost magical encounter among several characters on a bus in Havana. Throughout this section there are references to witchcraft and Afro-Cuban religious practices. In fact Cemí is on the bus returning home from a visit with a woman who calls herself a "visionary medium." The woman's name is Chacha, a pseudonym for Caridad, which in Cuba is related to the Virgin Patroness who is worshiped equally by Catholics and by those practicing the Afro-Cuban religion. This aspect of Cuban popular culture seems to be presented at this point in the novel so that Lezama can develop his poetic system from the standpoint of magic and fate. It was because of an extraordinary coincidence (Lezama calls it *azar concurrente*, or "the synchronicity of fate") that Oppiano Licario also appears on the same bus with Cemí and several other characters. Licario expresses the belief that our

---

* "un sujeto al sueño, sino, por el contrario, ya en el sueño, prolongarlo indefinidamente" (p. 425).

† "Ha vencido también el tiempo como *entre*, según la aceptación de algunos contemporáneos, pues en su sueño es imposible separar el tiempo que fue del que se está elaborando. Ese *entre* que parece ser el último refugio dialéctico de los mortales ... porque ese *entre* es la negación de toda penetración" (p. 426).

interpretations give form to the formless, and therefore we are "the artifice of a miracle" since we "have dominated the shapelessness of nature" (p. 442). This is his way of stating that poetry is the power to give substance to the chaos of nature.

The day after this fateful meeting, Cemí finds in his pocket a card from Licario inviting him to visit. On the card Cemí reads the phrase: "I knew your Uncle Alberto, I saw your father die," and thus Lezama establishes that Licario will stand as poetic substitution for the *lost father*. Cemí decides to visit Licario and walks toward the address indicated on the card. When he arrives at Licario's building he finds the light diffuse and cannot see clearly. While Cemí is groping about in an attempt to find the right apartment, Licario pounds on a table and cries out "*sistáltico* style." At this moment, several characters who happen to live in the same building as Licario begin a frenetic dance. Finally Cemí finds Licario, who now takes a small bronze triangle and, ringing it, exclaims: "*hesicástico* style." Cemí comments: "I see that you have moved in a short time from the *sistáltico* style, that of tumultuous passions, to the *hesicástico*, or that of a dynamic equilibrium."* Licario strikes the triangle again and says: "Then, we can begin" (p. 447). We cannot help but wonder what exactly is it that they can now begin. The answer to this question is that they can begin to create poetry, to write the novel that is writing them, and through this process begin the intended salvation of both the subject and the text. At the close of chapter 13, the novel starts to focus on the achievement of Cemí's development as the poet of the Image of the absence of natural order. His being, fragmented through crisis, has developed a complex poetic strategy in order to refamiliarize himself with the world. All that is lacking at this point is to specify Cemí's final strategy: his attempt to become reacquainted with language and with the text that is inventing him as the necessary fiction of a *dramatis personae*.

Oppiano Licario's view of the world and his relationship with Cemí are covered in the last chapter of the novel, which also recounts Cemí's success as a poet. It seems that even though Licario is a symbol of a very advanced stage of Lezama's poetics, he is not destined to arrive at Cemí's artistic perfection. Licario's

---

* "Veo ... que ha pasado del estilo sistáltico, o de las pasiones tumultuosas, al estilo hesicástico, o del equilibrio anímico, en muy breve tiempo."

metaphorical process does not completely encompass the area of the *supranatural* or its expression in language. His comparisons are established between common reality and memory, whereas Cemí succeeds in making comparisons between the event and its possible coinciding with the mysterious *supranature*. Licario's great contribution to Cemí in relation to his poetry is his conception of "morphological exceptions." It is to amplify and perfect this idea that Licario gives Cemí the *Compendium of Morphological Exceptions* (*Súmula de excepciones morfológicas*), a book that is a personal testament. What is meant by "morphological exceptions"? The text uses a gastronomic metaphor to explain the concept: if we take a traditional dish made with mincemeat and substitute pheasant for the mincemeat, we will have achieved "an exception that compares." In other words, we first establish the exception of exchanging something customary with something new, but the new element takes on meaning only in comparison with what it replaces: the pheasant is not only pheasant but also pheasant-in-place-of-mincemeat. The comparison has brought out the density of the signified. In this example, moreover, one can see in Licario's system of *comparative morphological exceptions* a certain amount of Gongorism, especially since he has substituted something "vulgar" (mincemeat) with something "genteel" (pheasant).[34]

Licario teaches Cemí that, given the void in nature, poetry finds an artifice that will replace this vacuum. Such an exchange is achieved through a comparison between something remembered and its substitution by a new artificial element. This contribution of Licario to the poetic system of the Image is connected directly with Cemí's father, the Colonel. Licario has come to help Cemí weave a system of relationships that will fill the vacuum left by the dead father (*Dead Nature*). Licario's metaphors take as their basis the comparison of the Morphological Elements of two things, common reality and memory, and then transcend to a third element, the poetic extension that remains as a trace of the previous comparison. The novel cites the following example from Goethe's *Theory of Colors* in order to emphasize the transition to the poetic level. Goethe glimpses, in the dim light of an inn, a pale girl dressed in scarlet. When she leaves, he sees on the wall a dark face surrounded by light, and the color of the clothes now seems to have a green tone. Licario's interpretation, considered in view of the theory of perception found in Goethe, seems to base itself in a double process: the attraction of the Image attempts the *act* of seeing the pale girl (in order to see the girl or anything else, one must begin with the power of making distinctions in the visible world); then, in her absence, there is a poetic regression that returns from the *act* to the *Image* that initially allowed the first vision. In the absence of the sensible, the creativity of the Image goes to work to permit a "substitute image" that acquires a poetic possibility. The first vision then extends itself to a third level, which Lezama calls the "knowing image" (pp. 458–59).

The novel also mentions Licario's sister, who plays a key role in Cemí's final stages of development as a poet by delivering to him the poem left by Licario just before his death. To meet her, Cemí must attend a wake held in honor of Licario. During his trip to the funeral home, Cemí finds himself involved in a nocturnal world of magical events and prodigious transformations. The very narration of this process is stately, ceremonial, and rich with mystery as if it were describing a Christian hero approaching the Holy Grail. All the elements of the fantastic discovered by Cemí on his way to the funeral home are interpreted by him within the context of extreme creativity. All seem to articulate signs of the *supranatural*, to be arrived at by an erotic-poetic penetration: "each clover represented a key, as if nature and the *supranatural* were united into something to penetrate, to jump from one region to the other, in order to arrive at the castle and interrupt the celebration of the secretive troubadours. A garland twined itself around Eros and Thanatos, the penetration of the vulva was the resurrection in the valley of splendor."* At this moment, Cemí's night vision glimpses the god Terminus, whose magnificent phallic proportions affirm again and again the relation between poetry and erotic incursion as a metaphor of penetration into the limitless possibilities of the Image.

Finally, arriving at Licario's wake, Cemí finds Licario's sister calling to him from the darkness. Ynaca Eco has the same confidence and sense of mystery about her that her brother exhibited.

---

* "cada trébol representaba una llave, como si se unieran la naturaleza y la sobrenaturaleza en algo hecho para penetrar, para saltar de una región a otra, para llegar al castillo e interrumpir la fiesta de los trovadores herméticos. Una guirnalda entrelazaba el Eros y el Tánatos, el sumergimiento en la vulva era la resurrección en el valle del esplendor" (p. 485).

She gives Cemí the poem Licario left to him, which expresses the confidence Licario had in Cemí and in his future achievements as a poet. It refers to poetry as the only possible testament after the body fades. Cemí, returning to his house in the middle of the night, is engrossed in poetic meditations, which cause him finally to exclaim "*hesicástico* rhythm, we can begin." This is the same phrase Licario had used the last time he was with Cemí. But since it is now Cemí who pronounces the phrase, it is Cemí who is now the poet, ready to begin the poem-novel that is *Paradiso.* Cemí is ready to begin to write the text that has been writing him and has reached its final words. This is the answer that the poet gives in his attempt to overcome the crisis of his fragmentation brought about by the absence of a natural order. It is also the way to bring about a reconciliation between the subject, the world, and writing.

If we again compare *Paradiso* with representative autobiographical novels, we begin to note that all the novelists after Wordsworth tend to develop the idea that the author's past contains the power to liberate the author from a weakened literary and spiritual condition. We also learn that a self-referential narration can assist in the process of liberation; and, finally, that the creative power of language can, by its representation of the past, transform the narrator. Nevertheless, this process also exposes the paradoxical difficulty of understanding how to restructure the psychological subject by modifying the structure of the literary subject through telling the "history of the subject in crisis." These contradictions grew ever more keen until Carlyle brilliantly captured the dilemma. In *Sartor Resartus,* Carlyle is explicit about the disparities that had begun to appear in Wordsworth's *Prelude* and manages to radically question the authenticity of autobiographical information.[35] Lezama continues, in a certain manner, on the path traced early on by Carlyle, a path that suggests the "autobiographical" text reflects only those spent fragments of *notions* concerning both the psychological and literary subject.

The philosophical articulation most relevant to a treatment of Carlyle's subject is found in Nietzsche, for whom the subject is never something given, but much more an entity discovered or invented. What is most curious here is the absence in Lezama of a consideration of a spiritual subject at one with God (as is found in Augustine), a romantic individual subject (as with Wordsworth), or even a Nietzschean secular subject with a totally disintegrated identity. Lezama is interested in a subject that, on the one side, creates and destroys by an evolutionary process, and on the other possesses a metaphorical memory that feeds on the creative energies of a transcending Image based upon the lack of natural order. So the Lezamian metaphor, with its attraction to the unknown depths of the Image and its propensity to penetrate these depths, provides an orientation for the metaphorical subject, which is a fundamental betterment of reality within a redeemed universe. Thus the Lezamian subject, contrary to the being-for-death of Heidegger, is much more a being-for-resurrection.[36]

In the novel *Paradiso*, Lezama weaves a character from autobiographical fragments that present an essentially fictionalized subject, and thus *Paradiso* is of the same family as Joyce's *Portrait* and Proust's *Remembrance of Time Past*. Lezama, like Joyce and Proust, systematizes the notion of both Carlyle and Nietzsche that literary self-representation is a form of self-fiction. More than simply remembering and re-presenting the subject of the past, Joyce, Proust, and Lezama favor a literary process that permits them to create an "other" conceived in the union of memory and imagination. Lezama's metaphorical subject, developed through the character José Cemí of *Paradiso*, comes about as the result of a new strategy addressing the problem of the dissimilarity between identity and discourse. This subject is actually a process, thus making more and more obvious the difficulty of transposing the psychological subject (the author) of an autobiographical text into a literary subject (the protagonist). In what way is José Cemí the author Lezama Lima or vice versa? The pseudo-autobiographical subject of *Paradiso* is the result of an increasing awareness of the complexities of such transposition. Lezama's poetics develops to the fullest a complex strategy designed to confront such a dilemma. The Image of the absence of natural order, with its power to consume differences, attempts to harmonize the distance between the name and the named, the subject and its representation. The Image presumes to embrace this enormous distance by founding itself on a negation that is total and antilogocentric. This void, in turn, opens new roads by way of its excessive negativity. By absorbing opposites, the Image presumes to expand and obliterate all differences.

José Lezama Lima, through the character José Cemí of *Paradiso*, presents himself as a subject in crisis seeking his "salvation" in a labyrinthine discourse in conflict with itself and with the identity of the psychological subject. José Cemí can only exist as the solution to the crisis brought about by the vocation of the "poet of the absence of natural order." Only by dealing with the history of the vocation of writer and poet can the fragmented subject in crisis hope to reinvent himself and start anew. Although the subject continues in a divided state, his only hope of unity and recovery is a self-invention brought about by a sort of exorcism of not only the personal, aesthetic, literary, and psychological, but also the historical. The sense of salvation in *Paradiso* and in all the works of Lezama must be understood in the context of an "imaginary history," which provides a "thread" with which the subject can construct a stable "nature." Moreover, we recall that in *Paradiso* a series of references to actual events of the Cuban Republic are given ample play. *Paradiso* not only is the imaginary story of José Lezama Lima's salvation, but also presumes to draw itself from the notions of a Cuban subject that is seeking a new "history" capable of redeeming him from his previous chaos and confusion.

Chapter 4

Poetry after the Storm

Oppiano Licario, Lezama's posthumous and unfinished novel,[1] is a continuation of the themes of *Paradiso*. But what is it that *Oppiano Licario* complements in relation to *Paradiso*? Its chief concern is the development of Lezama's poetics from a narrative perspective, which we have termed the poetics of the Image of an absent nature. In other words, *Oppiano Licario* continues the fictionalized expression of the possibilities that are born in the absence of natural order.[2] This general answer might be made more specific by noting that *Oppiano Licario* presents the search for, the loss of, and, in a certain manner, the recovery of Oppiano Licario's *Compendium of Morphological Exceptions*. Therefore Lezama's unfinished novel becomes the search for, the loss of, and the recovery of "The Book," "The Poem," "The Written Word." Furthermore, there are many instances within *Oppiano Licario* that elaborate upon essential points of Lezama's poetics, connecting threads that had remained at loose ends in his *Paradiso*.

That *Oppiano Licario* is a continuation of *Paradiso* is apparent at a variety of levels. For example, though new characters are introduced alongside those with whom we are familiar, many of these possess a haunting similarity to those of the first novel. The new characters appear as dramatic functions with the same basic characteristics as those of *Paradiso*, only now they are developing in new situations. This sense of relationship, similarity, and continuity is made explicit in the eighth chapter of *Oppiano Licario* when Fronesis, in a letter to Cemí, refers to the link connecting certain characters within the two novels: "All of them [the new characters in relation to those already known] contribute to the formulation of an intriguing constant among the generally fluctuating population."* The letter from Fronesis closes by noting: "If time is disregarded, this group now in Paris is the same as that evolved in the space and time of Havana."†

At its beginning, *Oppiano Licario* introduces a central theme: the absent father. It is clear from the first few lines that we are dealing with one of the more turbulent times in the history of

---

* "Todos ellos contribuyen a la formulación de una posible constante dentro de la población flotante" (p. 184).

† "Vaciado el tiempo, ahora ese grupo en París, es el mismo que se desenvolvía en un tiempo y un espacio habanero" (p. 184).

Cuba. The context for the theme of the absent father is the following episode: a death squad enters José Ramiro's house in order to arrest and kill him, subsequently leaving his widow and children destitute. After the conclusion of this violent episode, we find that José Ramiro was the neighbor of Dr. Fronesis, who "is the father of *our* Ricardo Fronesis." Here Lezama's use of *nuestro* (our) indicates that the reader is presumed to have read *Paradiso*.

Early in the narration, Lezama introduces a novelistic strategy that recurs frequently throughout *Oppiano Licario*: the sudden interruption of one episode in order to jump to another apparently unrelated one.[3] The most frequent interruption occurs between the narrations referring to Havana and those referring to Paris. We will find later, at the end of the novel (by taking into account the "outline" left by Lezama), that the worlds of Paris and Havana join to form one world, and what had seemed a series of unrelated, violent interruptions within the narrative flow becomes the far-reaching nexus that encompasses much of the complexity and significance of Lezama's fictionalization.

A great deal of the narration regarding Fronesis in Paris takes place in the apartment of the painter Champollion and his model Margaret, who is also a painter. It is through the observations of Margaret that the text begins to draw attention to the ambivalence of its own writing process and the difficulty of determining the line between writing as the process of damnation and that of salvation. She observes, "Writing provides a well of rebellion against damnation but is also itself a damnation, a god given to betraying gods and favoring mortals."* There are numerous clues throughout the text that place writing and the Image in a close relationship, but the strategy here is the *tokonoma*, a Japanese concept by which a flower is placed so as to bring alive the void, thereby bringing it to life. Just as Lezama's Image, the process of *tokonoma* creates from its absence (p. 23).[4] Lezama's Image is the absence that generates a figure, or metaphor, that unfolds, in turn, the creative process.

One constant theme in the novel is that of a positive force (love, friendship, the healthy erotic, etc.) in contrast with a negative one (hate, enmity, the maliciously erotic, etc.). Lezama

---

* "En la letra hay un fondo de rebeldía contra la maldición, pero también es ella una maldición, un dios dispuesto a traicionar a los dioses en favor de los mortales" (p. 21).

clearly indicates that the absence of a natural order can be filled by employing either of the polarities. For example, the loathing that Palmiro feels for Fronesis is an early instance of the destructive impulse dominating a vacuum: Palmiro colors with hate the absent image of Fronesis. In fact, one night Palmiro goes to Fronesis's house to kill him and stabs a cluster of pillows that he mistakes for the sleeping Fronesis. On the other hand, Margaret exemplifies the constructive drive occupying the void. Her paintings are said to be nothing more than "a search for the true face of her father," a man who had mistreated her. Now she "wants to draw this enemy from within [her]" (p. 21), and instead of attempting to kill her "enemy," as Palmiro does, she tries to rid herself of a negative image through the exorcism of her art.

The motif of exorcism through art is emblematized in *Oppiano Licario* by references to the work of Henry Rousseau and Pablo Picasso. In fact the first chapter ends with a series of conversations regarding the work of both painters. It is noted that Rousseau paints "in the modern manner," whereas Picasso follows "the way of the Egyptians." Rousseau is "modern" by virtue of his attention to detail and by "his marginal, yet joyous, sense of the totality of things." Moreover, "what he knows collides openly with what he does not know, yet what he does not know just as clearly enlivens what he does know—the characteristic of all powerful artists."* The nature of these opinions implies that Lezama identifies more readily with Rousseau than with Picasso, especially since most of his observations on the former apply equally to himself. It is within this context that the mention of Rousseau's paintings becomes an emblem for the art of Lezama's novel itself.[5]

While Champollion and Fronesis are discussing art, they are interrupted by the arrival of a young man named Cidi Galeb, whom Champollion characterizes as "very dangerous." Here, as well as throughout the novel, an analogy is drawn between Galeb and Foción that progressively reveals that, though they are similar in some ways, Galeb is actually the negative counterpoint to Foción. Galeb evolves into a symbol of the potential for corruption within the exceptional and, at another level, of the decadence and

---

* "... lo que conoce golpea en lo que desconoce, pero también lo que desconoce reacciona sobre lo que conoce, signo de todo artista poderoso" (p. 33).

decline of a marginal tradition. He is a descendant of a sultan from the imaginary eastern kingdom of Tupek and is in some way related to the Boabdil, the messengers who reported the fall of Granada to the Arab governors of Spain. Lezama's novel also includes a character who stands in opposition to Galeb: Mahomed, a rebel from the western kingdom of Tupek. Their relationship is one of complexity and tension. To further complicate matters, the novel, having established a mythical nexus between Galeb and Foción, also suggests an underlying relationship between Mahomed and Cemí.

In the last part of chapter 1 we are told that when Fronesis was with Galeb and Mahomed in a Paris cafe, a bomb exploded nearby, and both Galeb and Mahomed disappeared quickly. This episode can be read as a contrast to a similar instance in *Paradiso*, where, during the explosions of a student revolt at the University of Havana, both Fronesis and Foción rushed to help Cemí. In *Oppiano Licario*, the explosion prompts both Galeb and Mahomed to abandon Fronesis. It is one of those moments that might be taken as an instance of the dispersal that one critic considered characteristic of the first ten chapters.[6]

Another narrative interruption occurs in the second chapter, where there is a jump to a series of events taking place in Havana. Cemí, now at the university, is approached by Lucía, who tells him she is pregnant and that Fronesis is the father. She asks him to help her find enough money for a trip to Paris where she hopes to meet Fronesis. At this point the narration moves to Paris and relates a conversation between Mahomed and Fronesis in which Mahomed says that when he hears Fronesis speak, it is as if "[his] words carry us to the island" (p. 53).

From what Mahomed tells Fronesis of his life and ancestors, inferences can be drawn that connect Mahomed with Egyptian culture and the figure of Osiris, "who can procreate from the dead." In this way Lezama manages to relate Mahomed with a mythical figure who foreshadows both Christ and Orpheus, just as Mahomed frequently prefigures Cemí. Osiris is the Egyptian deity who most interests Lezama, a metaphor through which he explores the development of his poetic system, especially since Osiris is the only Egyptian god who manages to sow life even after his death. Although Lezama's Image is an absence related to the vacuum that is death, a spirit of salvation is always implied.

Death, for Lezama, contains the seeds of a kind of engendering. It is through this perception that Lezama's Image is closely related to Christian Resurrection: Resurrection conceived of as the absolute creativity of absolute death. Lezama often uses Osiris as a starting point for this perspective, as a figure whose death is involved with creation, then moves to Orpheus, a figure who returns from death carrying a flower, and finally to Christ, who redeems death itself, transforming the natural into the supernatural.

Foreshadowing the Image, Mahomed tells Fronesis: "I realized that my mother, my father, and I were, even then, nothing, our images having left only their shadows to pass from the finite of the mortals to the infinity of death. What I once called observation ... was the void and the image, death and continuity."* His vision insists on the elimination of the gap between the burden of a prodigious past and the vitality of a confused present. Only in this manner is it possible to arrive at the City of God. This, suggests the text, is a way to "hurry up the Resurrection" (p. 67).

The narration also explores the tragic tension between Fronesis and Galeb. Galeb clumsily attempts to seduce Fronesis from a context of hate and ill will, the opposite of Foción, whose erotic interest in Fronesis stems from his perception of Fronesis as a beautiful incarnation of friendship. The tension between Fronesis and Galeb allows the former to better understand both the kindness and dignity of Foción, who was an image of unfulfilled desire (p. 87). The image of Foción is associated with a final sense of the poetic image that goes beyond the carnal. The labyrinthine relationship of Fronesis and Foción is clarified in an episode in which Fronesis and Galeb find themselves sleeping in the same bed. As Galeb fondles Fronesis beneath the sheets, the latter dreams of being caressed by Foción. When Fronesis wakes up, he violently rejects Galeb's hand. The incident establishes a contrast between the rejected and the accepted hand, between the kind of desire that would steal upon the object in order to possess it and a love rich in the creative possibilities of the Image.

While those events are taking place in Paris, in Havana Op-

---

* "Sabía que mi madre, mi padre y mi yo éramos ya la nada, y que sólo las imágenes dejaban sus sombras al pasar de la finitud mortal a la infinitud de la muerte. Lo que yo había llamado observación ... eran la nada y la imagen, la muerte y la no interrupción" (p. 64).

piano Licario's first visit from beyond the grave is being narrated. Cemí and Licario encounter each other, and Cemí is entranced by the "mysterious energy of an Oppiano Licario ... who lives while dead and while dead is master of fabulous powers."* Licario thus takes his place within the constellation of those like Icarus, Osiris, Orpheus, and Christ, who, even in death, "sustained the same generative force they exhibited in life" (p. 100). Licario, like each of these mythic figures who serve as a mediation between the infinite and the finite, evokes the metaphorical process: "It was a metaphor capable of appearing at any moment within the infinite possibility of metaphor and analogy, since it seemed death had only augmented its ability to act by way of an extremely vigorous and unexpected image in the kingdom of the unconditional."†

The first four chapters of *Oppiano Licario* serve to establish the coordinates between characters that tend to be secondary and to prepare for the reappearance of Licario, but in the fifth chapter, the narration centers on Cemí and his encounter with Ynaca. We are told that Cemí went to Ynaca's house looking for her and found instead a house filled with spiderwebs. The subtext of this episode stresses the analogy between the spider and its web and the poet and his or her poetry: the spider, as the poet, weaves interconnecting threads across a vacuum and brings about "an infinite approximation of the figure and the image" (p. 113). Afterward, Cemí goes to the library of the Castle of Force (Castillo de la Fuerza), where, as if by magic, he comes across Ynaca. This strange encounter is, among other things, a manner of celebration for Oppiano Licario's return from the dead; we are told that their meeting means that Oppiano "has been resurrected" (p. 118).

For Cemí, the figure of the resurrected Licario is related to "gnostic space" (p. 121). Yet, Licario, attracted by this empty space, speaks from the perspective of the dead and the exceptional. Cemí, however, as the true poet, attempts to translate the *supranatural* into the natural. He deliberately tries to "trap" the

---

* "Percibía la impulsión misteriosa de Licario ... que había vivido en la muerte, y que ya muerto era dueño de fabulosos recursos" (p. 95).

† "Era una metáfora que en cualquier momento podía surgir, el infinito posible análogo de la metáfora, pues parecía que la muerte aumentaba más su posibilidad de actuar sobre una imagen extremadamente vigorosa e inesperada en el reino de lo incondicionado" (p. 102).

infinity of the Image through metaphorical comparisons. Through this process, Cemí completes the poetics of Licario, and his system merges the finite with the infinite and the reverse. With this in mind, I suggest that one of the keys to the novel can be found in the following passage that Ynaca relates to Cemí:

Do not fear anything, Licario told me frequently: he has what we lack. Then he continued: I have come to it very late. Death is near. But the two of you need to know this while you are young. Yet he never said what it was we lacked and what it was you alone possessed. Learn to know him, he would tell me repeatedly. He will be your most valued source of knowledge. At his death, Licario believed he had lived for two things: that he had come to know you, and that the two of us would come to know one another. Now, the three of us can rest content. He can now sing a cantata as rich as those of Bach: we are not alone in death. And we, in turn, can sing after the manner of Handel that we are also not alone in life. It is an anticipation of the Resurrection when both the living and the dead will be judged. I know through Licario and hold it as a sacred order that the only thing I lack is a knowledge of you. Licario sought it by attempting to befriend your Uncle Alberto and the Colonel. But he arrived at the party too late. Alberto and the Colonel escaped him through death. He spoke to you no more than four or five times but it was sufficient for him to determine that you understood through the image, just as he understood by way of morphological exceptions. If ever the three of us coordinate our work, agree fully on this issue, I recall that he told me, on one of the last occasions I spoke with him, that this would mean the end of the world.*

---

* "No se asuste, pues Licario me decía con fecuencia: él tiene lo que a nosotros nos falta. Después añadía: yo lo he conocido demasiado tarde, la muerte está cerca, pero tú debes conocerlo en la juventud de los dos. Pero nunca me dijo qué era lo que nos faltaba y qué era lo que usted tenía. Conocerlo a él, será tu mejor fuente de conocimiento, me repetía. Al morir Licario creyó que su vida se había logrado por dos motivos: porque al fin lo había conocido a usted y porque nosotros dos nos conoceríamos. Ahora, los tres podemos estar contentos. Él puede entonar una cantata que puede ser de Bach: no estamos solos en la muerte. A la que podemos contestar con otra cantata que puede ser de Haendel: no estamos solos en la vida. Es un

The purpose of the relationship between Ynaca and Cemí is to conceive a child (we later find out it is a girl) who will symbolize the incarnation of the Image as a metaphor. Yet despite the religious overtones, we are not concerned here with a mystical system that would spiritualize the corporeal. In fact the motive is in a certain way the exact opposite: the incorporation of the possibilities of the void. Thus, regardless of the long, convoluted conversations between them, the "function" of Cemí and Ynaca is to make love and engender a new life. To have failed in this would mean being unable to convert the *supranatural* to the natural and vice versa. Lezama's system demands that the poet make of the *supranatural* the natural, bring poetry to the poem. The here and now is like a weight that falls toward the corporeal. In this way Lezama's system incorporates Time as providing the context of continuity within which the fragments of the here and now secure the possibilities of the Image (p. 126). In one of his talks with Ynaca, Cemí explains his conception of Time as the "uncreated creative" (p. 131). The chapter ends when Ynaca hands over to Cemí the *Compendium of Morphological Exceptions* written by Licario, advising him that he is now charged with the "tragic responsibility" of guarding this work.

The great tragedy of the novel is related in the sixth chapter: a huge storm settles over Havana, and the winds and the rain disperse the pages of Licario's *Compendium*. The manuscript was over two hundred pages, with an eight- or nine-page poem as its centerpiece. It was, according to the novel, not only a "compendium of exceptions" but also the Book, the Mirror, and the Key. The text indicates Licario's relation to his work when it says: "Of the book's title, the reason for his life [Licario's] was the search for these morphological exceptions. He knew the vibrating force, the vacuum and its reinforcement, this empty space ejected by the ex-

anticipo de la resurrección, pues él juzgará a los vivos y a los muertos. Por Licario sé, y eso es para mí como una orden sagrada, que lo que me falta sólo podré conocerlo en usted. Licario lo buscó queriendo amigarse con su tío Alberto y con el Coronel, pero llegaba tarde a la fiesta. Esas personas se le escapaban hacia la muerte. A usted le habló cuatro o cinco veces, las suficientes para saber si usted conocería por la imagen y él por las excepciones morfológicas. Si los tres trabajásemos juntos o puestos de acuerdo, recuerdo que me dijo una de las últimas veces que hablé con él, sería el fin del mundo" (p. 121).

pansion of the forces of cohesion, which blossoms and greets us, making of the two of us one."*

Without doubt, the *Compendium* was a text whose beauty consisted in suggesting a harmony between the "I" and its secret circumstances, produced by relating that "I" with the unknown through exceptional situations. To lose Licario's text was to be deprived a sense of meaning drawn from the unknown. The "I" seeks to salvage creative energy from the midst of the unknown that threatens us with an all-encompassing death. It is precisely this excess, this destructive force, that the poet must confront and from it draw the possibilities of poetry. The poet's role is one of continual renewal, giving a positive answer in the face of the threats of the void (p. 149).

The process of creation drawn from an infinity of nothingness is presented symbolically by treating the loss of the manuscript, the storm, and the moment of conception by Ynaca as simultaneous events. Leaving Ynaca, Cemí returns home to find that a Caribbean cyclone has scattered the pages of the *Compendium*. All that remains is an "indecipherable text," which consists of nothing more than the "poem situated within the prose" (p. 155).

The events of the storm in Havana happen at the same time that the narration relates Lucía's meeting with Fronesis, during which she informs him that Lucía is pregnant. The seventh chapter also includes several episodes concerning Galeb's relationships with those characters who are in Paris. This series of encounters and characterizations serves to call attention to Galeb, who, as we see later, is responsible for the assassination of Fronesis. Galeb is the symbol of the destructive force that Lucía, Cemí, and Foción all sense whenever Fronesis's future is considered. Since the assassination of Fronesis does not occur in the ten chapters left by Lezama, it would be impossible to consider the event in the overall scheme of the novel without reading the "outline" left by the author. Through this "outline" we are able to better our judgment and grasp a more complete idea of Lezama's plan for the work.

The progressive movement of the novel toward an ever-in-

---

* "Del título de su obra, la justificación de su vida fue la búsqueda de esas excepciones morfológicas, él sabía que la fuerza vibratoria, ese vacío y ese refuerzo, el espacio vacío desalojado por la expansión de la fuerza cohesiva, que aflora y nos da la mano, haciendo una pareja" (pp. 144–45).

creasing relationship between the worlds of Paris and Havana is brought about by means of letters exchanged among characters and their trips between the two cities. For example, we are told in chapter 7 that Ynaca has come to Paris and has visited Fronesis. During their meeting, Fronesis finds out a number of subtle elaborations regarding the poetic objectives of Licario. The eighth chapter emphasizes that Cemí's friendship with Licario has allowed him to unify the image with knowledge and that his union with Ynaca was the joining of knowledge with erotic love. It is in this chapter that Fronesis receives a letter from Cemí, in response to one of his own. Cemí tells of the storm and the loss of the manuscript, as well as something of his relationship with Ynaca. Thus, albeit tangentially, Fronesis is included within the seminal actions of the novel. Moreover, for the first time the reader learns that Cemí has found four pages of the poem in the middle of Licario's text. Cemí includes the fragment in his letter to Fronesis in hopes of "its possible reconstruction" (p. 185). Additionally, an "editorial" note at the foot of the page indicates that "the poem to which the text refers does not exist in the original manuscript" (p. 185). The "note" can be interpreted as intended to confuse the reader, since the mentioned poem cannot be read. Thus the reader, like Cemí and Fronesis, is included in a form of quest for the lost text. Everyone now becomes involved in a process of reconstruction and interpretation within a vacuum.

In this section of the novel, we also encounter the episode of a fortune-teller who lives with a "half-crazy teenager." The meeting between Fronesis and the adolescent seems to hold little significance within the overall structure of the novel unless one knows that for Lezama, true poetry is always associated with a kind of necessary madness. The teenager maintains that he must live in the same house as the fortune-teller to participate in the mystery of poetry (p. 194). He then adds:

The most powerful resource that man has is losing its meaning, its knowledge, its magic, its health, all of which has converted him into a vulgarity of the immediate. It is still possible to speak with you about these things that are in the body of man, a thing now very rare in Havana and, for that matter, in Paris. And since man has lost his body, he has also denied the Image. Yet there is nothing more than the body of the image and the image of the body. Ultimately, the image creates us and our body secretes the image, just as the snail's shell secretes forms within a frozen spiral. This is the silent heaven of the Tao. Just as for Descartes there is nothing beyond thought and extension, for me there is nothing beyond body and image. This can only be captured through poetry. That is why I remain beside myself when confronted with the inferiority that marks these times we suffer and cry out within.... Poetry must embrace difficulty, must celebrate the great victory of our hidden forces over the present mediocrity of man.... We must return to a definition of God by way of poetry.*

The extremely dramatic ninth chapter begins in Havana with Foción thinking of Fronesis. Apparently agitated by the absence of the latter, Foción throws himself from Havana's seawall and is attacked by a shark. A swimmer rescues him and kills the shark with a knife. Since Foción has been bitten on the arm, the swimmer tows him ashore. We are also told that Dr. Fronesis (Fronesis's father) has had a heart attack. Dr. Fronesis's attack is the consequence of a note from Lucía reporting that Fronesis has been wounded in Paris. As the auto carrying Dr. Fronesis approaches Havana's seawall, it is slowed by the group taking care of the wounded Foción. Dr. Fronesis insists that the driver place Foción in the car with him and that they be driven to a doctor. As a final instance of almost magic coincidence, the doctor whom they visit is none other than Foción's crazy father

---

* "El más poderoso recurso que el hombre tiene ha ido perdiendo significación profunda, de conocimiento, de magia, de salud, para convertirse en una grosería de lo inmediato. Todavía se puede hablar con usted de estas cosas que están en el cuerpo del hombre, y eso es tan raro ya en La Habana como en París, pues así como el hombre ha perdido su cuerpo, también se le niega la imagen. Y no hay nada más que el cuerpo de la imagen y la imagen del cuerpo. La imagen al fin crea nuestro cuerpo y el cuerpo segrega imagen, como el caracol segrega formas en espiral inmóvil, que es el cielo silencioso de los taoístas. Así como para Descartes no hay más que pensamiento y extensión, para mí no hay nada más que cuerpo e imagen. Y lo único que puede captarlo es la poesía y por eso me desespero ante la inferioridad que la recorre en los tiempos que sufrimos y lloramos.... Hay que llevar la poesía a la gran dificultad, a la gran victoria que partiendo de las potencias oscuras venza lo intermedio en el hombre.... Hay que volver a definir a Dios partiendo de la poesía" (pp. 194–95).

whose medical practice consists more of magic than of medicine. He decides to mix the blood of Dr. Fronesis and Foción and make of this a healing potion. The first to show improvement as a result of this cure is Dr. Fronesis, who asks that as soon as Foción gets better, he be told of the wounding of Fronesis in Paris. Dr. Fronesis wants Foción to go to Paris to see Fronesis, believing that this is the surest way to guarantee his son's recovery. Here we begin to realize that all these events in the novel serve to unite several characters who up to now were enemies. The narration is heading toward a great metaphor of reconciliation.

This hectic episode is narrated in sequences, interrupted by a series of narratives referring to Fronesis in Paris and his thoughts about Foción. Fronesis, for example, discovers through conversation with a fortune-teller that he has come to Paris to find his mother. This discovery suggests the theme of *American Expression*, which recurs throughout the work of Lezama Lima. Europe is presented as one of the principal cultures among those that nurture the New World. Fronesis, the American, is going to know his European mother and thus know himself better. His actions show an increasing "Cubanization" of European culture, and on one occasion, when he sees a library with shelves made of Cuban wood, he experiences "the revelation that this accumulation of knowledge must be returned to Cuba, to the hidden center, to the unknown" (p. 211).

The theme of *American Expression* recurs at the close of the chapter, where in a dream Foción "rides a shark into Europe." Furthermore, continuing the emphasis upon the relationship between Europe and America, the dream contains a reference to the myth of Taurus. Foción imagines that "a bull draped in garlands comes to receive him with snortings that sound like laughter" (p. 218). (See chapter 5 of the present volume for an analysis of the metaphor.) We know from Lezama's essays that within his poetic system of the world, American culture is born of a mix of many cultures in decomposition, including that of Europe. Lezama's system frequently refers to the revitalization of European culture in the context of the New World, and his symbol is Taurus the bull. After raping Europa in order to engender culture, he abandons her and leaves for the New World, where he is greeted with wreaths and garlands and sings anew in a rich, lusty baritone. There is no doubt that both Fronesis and Foción are playing dual roles: these roles relate not only to the Lezamian conception of poetry but also to his vision of American culture. While in Paris, Fronesis not only searches for his European mother but also thinks of Cuba when he contemplates the library shelves made of Cuban wood. And Foción dreams that his arrival in Europe is heralded by none other than the culture-bearing bull.

The fortune-teller advises Fronesis that his trip to Europe is something beyond the quest for his mother. She tells him, "what you will also be involved in is the reconstruction of a manuscript called the *Compendium of Morphological Exceptions*" (p. 209).[7] Thus the role of Fronesis is affirmed as one of the instruments through which Cemí, by the process of evaluation and assessment, will reconstruct the lost writing of the sacred book. Fronesis's life becomes one of the models that Cemí must emulate (at least for the time being) in order to reconstruct certain areas of the book. Fronesis becomes, then, an addition of Licario's doctrine in those areas where that doctrine involves ethical action.

Foción, having recovered from the shark wound, decides to follow the advice of Dr. Fronesis and go to Europe. He travels with his son, Focioncillo, but instead of proceeding directly to France, the two of them enter Europe by way of Italy. Lezama elects to characterize each culture the pair encounters by emphasizing the manner in which the museum guards attend to Focioncillo's comical and insistent desire to "take a piss" each time he finds himself in front of a piece of European art. The Italian guard, after taking Focioncillo to an ancient bathroom, insists that Foción give him a tip. At the Prado, Focioncillo is treated courteously, and the guard asks for nothing. The guard at the British Museum is simply cold and correct. The visit to the British Museum allows Lezama to make yet another point in his cultural characterization. Focioncillo notices that in the English paintings there are only blond children, which prompts the following observation: "Daddy, all these kids are blond. I could never be in one of these." It is an instance of marked cultural contrast. Foción answers: "If you were to conjure up a strong wind, perhaps a cyclone, you too could walk in these gardens" (p. 223). The context suggests that the metaphor of the cyclone, as well as being able to destroy and scatter the sacred book of Licario, can also assume the function of the type of force capable of rearranging the cultural universe and thus permitting the assimilation of other cultures.

Lezama's manuscript breaks off abruptly, just as Ynaca and her impotent husband, Abatón, receive an invitation to a party at McCormack's house. From this point on we have no choice but to rely heavily on Lezama's "outline" of the unfinished novel. According to this "outline," Fronesis will be assassinated coincidentally with Cidi Galeb's arrival in Havana. In addition, Foción will kill Galeb to avenge the murder of Fronesis, then commit suicide. This series of events thus associate Foción's death with that of Fronesis. Furthermore, we find Lucía has a son, and Ynaca a daughter. Focioncillo, the son of Foción, must be included here among the children of the principal characters, even though he appears in the completed part of the novel. It also seems clear that Lezama intended to introduce a series of growing relationships among these children. This supposition is confirmed by means of the "outline," as well as by an interview with Lezama held by Reynaldo González in 1972.[8]

We also find in the "outline" that though the cyclone has destroyed the manuscript left by Licario, Abatón has acquired a copy of the *Compendium*. We are also told that the *Compendium* sets forth in writing all that has transpired in *Oppiano Licario* (whose original title, we learn, was *Inferno*) and includes the complex relationships of the children of Cemí, Fronesis, and Foción. The implication here is that the *Compendium* is *almost* the same book as the one we have been reading. A further implication is that, notwithstanding that the manuscript is the work of Licario, the poet of the exceptional, there is no way it can coincide perfectly with the work of Cemí, the poet of the Image. Cemí manages to read the copy of the *Compendium* held by Abatón and thus anticipates and frustrates the Goethean resolution that would have been symbolized by the marriage of his daughter with Fronesis's son. The "outline" reads: "Cemí prevents his daughter from traveling to Europe where she might encounter the son of Fronesis. He does this in order to prevent the recurrence of the myth of Euphorion.... Cemí's daughter marries the son of Foción"*[9] This marriage means, according to Lezama's poetic view, the union of the image with madness.

---

* "Cemí impide que su hija vaya a Europa, para que no se encuentre con el hijo de Fronesis. Para evitar el mito de Euforión. Se casan la hija de Cemí con el hijo de Foción."

In this manner the novel refers to one of the "solutions" of the poetic system of the world: the interwoven relationship between the metaphorical subject (Narcissus) and madness (Cassandra). Lezama's poetics always points toward the breaking of limits of reason. Poetry, as a form of the mad cries of Cassandra directed toward Apollo (the god of reason) who imprisoned her, is a figure that exists within the space of the nonrational. This poetry is born out of the vacuum created by a lack of natural order. Yet this void always contains within it the redemptive power of the Image, which, in turn, functions as the magnetic force capable of drawing the dispersed fragments into a redeemed whole.

In sum, we can only note that *Oppiano Licario* continues and complements the complex poetics of *Paradiso*. The sustaining motif is the acquisition, loss, and recovery by Cemí of the *Compendium of Morphological Exceptions*. It is significant that Cemí receives the manuscript from Ynaca, Licario's sister, who warns him that it is a sacred book that exceeds the limits of the known and of the unknown. It is Cemí's task to assimilate the work of Licario and move beyond the older poet's vision by appending the poetics of the Image. When the manuscript is lost in a storm, Cemí must revert to a complex poetic strategy in order to bring about its recovery. This involves an interpretation of Fronesis's life and, finally, the recovery of the *copy* of the manuscript that Abatón has been holding. Cemí's intercourse with Ynaca and the birth of his daughter are components of the overall strategy that will lead toward the "recovery" of the lost text. This daughter is a symbol of the possibility that exists when the poetics of the exceptional is united with the poetics of the Image. However, it seems Lezama wishes to complete his vision by the addition of yet another element. Thus the marriage of Cemí's daughter with Foción's son suggests that for Lezama it is always necessary that poetic discourse be wed to the discourse of madness. Focioncillo can be considered the son of the madman, recalling the previously discussed relationship between metaphoric subject (Narcissus) and poetic-mad discourse (Cassandra). The key to the poetics of Lezama remains the potential of the Image, which serves as the magnet drawing together and giving form to the fragments of the exceptional.

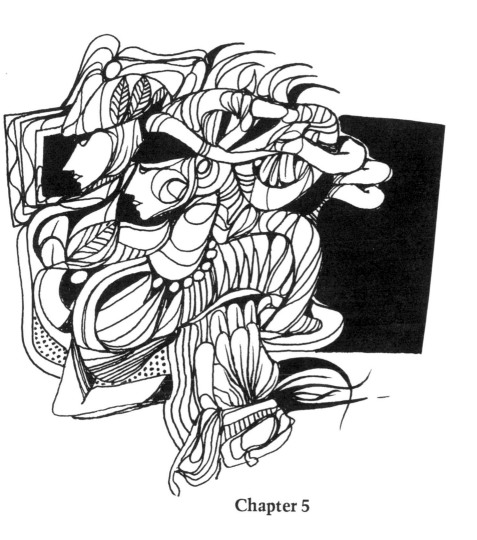

Chapter 5

The New Shores of Taurus

L ezama believes that a European culture in decline could be revived by cultural renovation from the New World, especially by that movement we know today as the Spanish American baroque. He shares with his compatriot and contemporary Alejo Carpentier a vision of Latin America as the continent upon which the baroque sensibility exercises a new and profound cultural impulse. It is a sense of the baroque that manifests itself not only in art but also in nature—an idea that coincides with thoughts brought forth in Oswald Spengler's *The Decline of the West*, a work well-known to Lezama as well as to the majority of the intellectuals of his generation.[1] Spengler notes that history has never produced one culture with the capacity to dominate the entire scientific and artistic expression, but rather, at any given time there exist various cultures in different stages of development. Since Spengler found within these cultures a cycle of birth, growth, aging, and eventual disappearance, like the patterns of a living organism, he formed his ideas around a biological metaphor. It was this Spenglerian concept that gave importance to those cultures at the margins of the so-called center of Western tradition. These "peripheral" societies received from him a kind of theoretical validity. Latin America, as a continent comprising a multitude of cultures, eagerly accepted this recognition of its values.

The diversity of cultures is one of the specific, fundamental factors in the development of the uniquely Latin American baroque. This was postulated not only by Lezama but also by Carpentier, who viewed Latin America as the natural environment for baroque proliferation owing to the cultural mix and the symbiosis and intermingling of races. These elements resulted in a style without a style that, by the very nature of its variety, appears amorphous—precisely one of the characteristics of the baroque sensibility.[2]

For his part, Lezama also believed that Latin America would realize itself in a dazzling fusion of races and cultures. He considered the Eurocentric point of view and any sense of Latin American inferiority in comparison to Europe as unacceptable. The Latin American, by incorporating elements of European culture, would transform them into significant new statements, into a new culture. For Lezama, history functions like a myth or a poem: the memory of a past act is transformed into a new image, and poetic memory is a kind of stage where the past takes on new life at an imaginary level. To imagine past acts is to allow the Image to present them as *dramatis personae* at another level. To name them implies the destruction of their memory and their reconstruction in another dimension of the imagination. This is Lezama's conception not only of poetry but also of history in general and of the history and culture of Latin America in particular. He expresses this view in his "The Possible Images" ("Las imágenes posibles"):

> Europe created culture, its particular brand, with characters who claim Greek dialectics, Bach's choruses, German idealist metaphysics, Dostoevski, the French novel of the nineteenth century. These we have converted to *dramatis personae*. They dance through the image that has destroyed them, with only a name. There is no river: we say river or the sea, and we open a curtain and the sea appears. The individual, the person, the mask, the embroidery, all are already in another dimension.[*3]

Following on this thought, Lezama developed the metaphor of the Bull (Taurus) as the image of the force that, by raping Europa, brought about her fecundity. Now, however, he has abandoned the pale European world of abstraction and crossed the sea in order to seek "a new love" in the New World:

> Taurus ... has always been weak when it comes to the pallor and abstraction of Europa.... But the bull, who also has his baritone guffaw, began to walk toward the sea, then toward the sea with night. Europa dragged herself to the high ridge above dry land and, despite the danger of falling, began to scream. The bull, the old lover of her pallor and abstraction, continued toward the sea with night, and Europa was thrown over the

---

* "Europa creó la cultura, una segregación suya, con personajes que claman la dialéctica griega, la coral bachiana, la metafísica idealista alemana, Dostoyeski, la novela francesa del siglo XIX. Los hemos convertido en *Dramatis personae;* a través de la imagen que los ha destruido, danzan, con solo un nombre, no hay un río, se dice un río, o el mar, y se descorre una cortina y aparece el mar. El individuo, la persona, la máscara, la mascarilla, ya están en otra dimensión."

quicksands, puffed up and tattooed: be careful, I've made the culture. Among the cries we remember: the god Pan has died, the Nietzschean "I have killed God," and the evening editions shouted their headlines: Europa has been assassinated, in a little pocket of her handbag they've found culture.... Europa, with her pallor and her abstraction, is alone on the beach. The Afghan novel is not there. Neither is an American metaphysics. Europa made culture. And that line: "We need to feign hunger when we steal the fruit." A feigned hunger? Is that what remains to the Americans? Though we are not in harmony, nor daydreaming, nor intoxicated nor anticipating: the bull has entered the sea, he has shaken off the pallor and the abstraction, and we can hear his deep-throated, baritone laugh as he receives flowers in the shores while his hoof scratches the skin of a new love.*[4]

To explain the formation of a new culture, Lezama brings into play another idea that coincides with Spengler's view: *each culture is mythically rooted in the landscape in which it has developed.*[5] However, the Cuban author modifies the corollaries of this idea to such an extent that he arrives at conclusions entirely different from those of Spengler. In *The Decline of the West*, a relationship is established between landscape, culture, and history, which serves Spengler as a point of departure for his world view.

---

* "Taurus ... siempre ha sido débil con la blancura, con la abstracción de Europa.... Pero el toro, que también tiene su risotada baritonal, comenzó a caminar hacia el mar, luego hacia el mar con noche. Europa arrastraba su cuerpo hacia el lomo sin agua, aunque pudiera caerse. Y Europa comenzó a gritar. El toro, antiguo amante de su blancura, de su abstracción, siguió hacia el mar con noche, y Europa fue lanzada sobre los arenales, hinchada con un tatuaje en su lomo sin tacha: tened cuidado, he hecho la cultura. De los gritos que recordamos: el Dios Pan ha muerto, el nietzscheano he matado a Dios, y las ediciones vespertinas que voceaban: el asesinato de Europa, en el bolsón de su faltriquera se ha encontrado la cultura.... Europa con su blancura y su abstracción está sola en la playa. No hay la novela de Afganistán ni la metafísica americana. Europa hizo la cultura. Y aquel verso: 'tenemos que fingir hambre cuando robemos los frutos.' ¡Hambre fingida? ¡Es eso lo que nos queda a los americanos? Aunque no estemos en armonía ni en ensueño, ni embriaguez o preludio: el toro ha entrado en el mar, se ha sacudido la blancura y la abstracción, y se puede oír su acompasada risotada baritonal, recibe otras flores en la orilla, mientras la uña de su cuerpo raspa la corteza de una nueva amistad."

For Spengler, each culture has roots in a specific landscape and is defined as the spiritual orientation of a human group that has come to a certain mutually agreed-upon conception of the world. This agreed-upon world view is expressed in a manner peculiar to and greatly influenced by the physical space in which the members of the group live out their lives. But the point must be made here that Lezama always implies an ongoing transcendence of the human subject and an unceasing pattern of historical unfolding that is directed toward a fundamental betterment of all of Creation. His view is in contrast to Spengler's cyclical conception of culture that rules out the idea of historical progress.

For Spengler, landscape and physical space function as the basic symbol that is the key to a specific historical understanding. With his "decentralized" sense of history, Spengler resembles a kind of Kepler of the philosophy of culture. History, like the stars, falls from a pure center or absolute point of reference and thus can only be traced elliptically, not in a linear fashion. Since each culture creates its own image, history is thus multiform and resembles a baroque fiction, which consists of a series of cultural configurations out of touch with one another. Within this conception, Western Europe is only *one* among many independent cultural entities. From this perspective, through the study of history one can only attempt a comparison of the morphologies of diverse cultures; such a comparison is difficult to justify since it deals with isolated societies that have no mutual points of reference.[6] Apart from these theoretical difficulties, Spengler offers yet another problem for a Latin American such as Lezama, who sought direction in history and hoped for cultural betterment. For Spengler, there was no historical objective: his history lacks meaning since it consists solely of isolated cycles. Therefore Lezama, seeking something more from history, chooses to explore other theoretical possibilities.

Carpentier developed a conception of history similar to Lezama's regarding the relationship between landscape and culture, and often affirmed that Latin America was always baroque, not only by the symbiosis of many races but also by virtue of its extraordinarily abundant nature. The "magic realism," which fuses with the baroque "substance" of Latin American nature, thrives in America because there the real *is* magic. Latin Americans write in the baroque style because the continent itself *is* baroque.[7]

Although Carpentier never fully rejected Spengler, he did considerably modify many of his own ideas during his lifetime. The movement of Carpentier's thought can be traced from a position very near that of Spengler to a later position closer to that of Vico, Hegel, Sartre (in his *Critique of Dialectical Reason*), and Marx.[8] Carpentier emphatically denies that the baroque is decadent and explains with a wealth of detail how it often appears in moments of transition and at times of crisis. Therefore the baroque, far from being decadent, is a "creative resource" that reappears in the history of artistic manifestations. Carpentier maintains that it is not a historical style but a "creative spirit." The "baroque spirit" arose before and showed up after the epoch that bears its name. Furthermore, Carpentier considers the baroque to be a spiritual constant born as a sharp reaction to the emptiness that characterizes those periods of brusque contrasts. It manifests itself in an art that leaves no space untouched, which rejects harmony, avoids the geometric and the linear forms, and seeks the off-centered. In addition, it favors the multiplication of disconnected elements of an organic continuum while aspiring to motion and unceasing rupture. All these characteristics coincide, in the opinion of Carpentier, with Latin American reality. Classicism, to the contrary, is dominated by harmony and a sense of a centered universe and emerges when a culture is fully secure with a homogeneous conception of itself. It opposes the breaking of form, progress, change, and revolution.[9]

Lezama Lima's *The American Expression* (*La expresión americana*) takes up Carpentier's vision of culture, history, and landscape. In this series of essays, Lezama—apart from noting the cultural exhaustion of Europe and positing the New World as the salvation of a fading culture—elaborates on the distinctions between European and American baroque.[10] The European baroque is characterized by an accumulation of elements, but also by a lack of great tension and asymmetry. It thus avoids the extreme fragmentation of elements in the same cultural unit: it is a baroque that has not forgotten the gothic.[11] However, the Latin American baroque feeds on tension and fragmentation, owing more than anything else to the social diversity that inevitably breaks up cultural units in order to weld them together into a new creation.

Yet despite the fact that Lezama and Carpentier share a view of the baroque, their differences are considerable. Perhaps the greatest difference is seen in their respective views on the foundation of the concept of culture and consequently the foundation of the baroque. Even though both agree that cultural diversity and landscape are the roots of a culture, each offers a different interpretation of the transcendence of the human subject as a mediator between landscape and history. For Carpentier, the human subject is the intermediary between these two elements, but the subject's act of transcendence has no religious meaning, as it does for Lezama.[12] Carpentier's subject wishes to arrive at a place determined by the aspirations of this world. Carpentier often gives socioeconomic and contextual reasons as an explanation for the collective conscience of a people, such as when he proposes that the beginning of Cuban culture was associated with activities during the end of the eighteenth and the beginning of the nineteenth centuries. Following the Haitian revolution, Cuba experienced a dramatic increase in black slavery and the growth of the sugar industry.[13] Carpentier sees history as an unfolding, an evolution toward "a something better," which is essentially human in nature.

Even though Lezama includes a historical projection that is realized at the human level, he develops a global, teleological vision based upon an elaborate concept of the *supranatural* Image. Landscape constitutes an image for the human group that inhabits it, and since this landscape comes to acquire meaning and involves itself in the formation of a culture, it must be interpreted by a "metaphorical human subject."[14] Once the image of geographic space is perceived within this context, the human subject relates this image with all the elements of his or her universe, and the historical vision of this particular culture arises as a result of reflecting on this process.[15] Thus, for Lezama, historical vision is not based on some unique moment of origin, some pure source from which all history flows—such as Carpentier sought in *The Lost Steps*. Rather, it comes about through a regressive projection that compares two imaginary forms: a sensory present reality and a remembrance of an invisible reality. The subject's interpretation, which mediates between these two forms, functions metaphorically. The subject compares something known with something unknown, a visible form with one that is invisible, and it is this process of metaphorical memory that provides the human subject and culture with a vision of his or her trajectory in Time.[16] For Lezama, this is an "imaginary" process by which the human subject interprets the image of the landscape.

Lezama assures us that within the context of this "imaginary" vision there cannot exist any repetition of identical configurations or historical periods. History always continues its process of *becoming* history.[17] What can survive is the basic image of a culture. Therefore, instead of persisting in the concept of culture as expressed by Spengler, Lezama develops the idea of "imaginary eras" (*"eras imaginarias"*), drawn from a transcendental vision of the human subject, and from a history that is the Image realizing itself metaphorically in Time. This view is similar to Giambattista Vico's, who saw history as the process of Providence expressing itself in a spiral movement that affirms historical progression. The constant gyrating is done in a progressive pattern owing to the tension between past and future.[18] For Vico, the advance of history is measured by the extent to which the plebeians acquire the rights and privileges of the patricians who once held them in bondage. It is not at all difficult to see in this the reason that Vico, for all his Catholic providentialism, was an influence on both Hegel and Marx. What draws a modern thinker to Vico's philosophy is the fact that he was the first to elaborate a profound anti-Cartesian system of historical meaning.[19] In addition, his theories present, among other things, an example of class struggle, historical cycles that progress toward human freedom, and a conception of a historical human subject directly opposed to the *cogito* of Descartes. According to Vico, the nature of the human subject is not static but historical, and each age functions within the confines of an image of itself, which, in turn, is used to interpret the universe from its specific perspective. Vico also anticipated the idea of an economic class structure as a crucial element in the formation of the modern world, characterized by a lack of common culture and of a sense of the whole.

Vico's *The New Science* addresses the fragmentation of the modern technological world, which, as he points out, associates this with the decadence of modernity. This division is the product of the "barbarism" of reflexive thought that has lost touch with the richness of the imagination.[20] The word "barbarism" implies that the human subject has lost a sense of unity within his or her own image, and certainly this is one of the possible meanings of

Lezama's first great poem, "Death of Narcissus." On the one hand it suggests the fragmentation of the image of the modern human subject, and on the other it includes the possibility of the reconstruction of this image in an imaginary sphere. The poem gives a total vision through which Narcissus dies in order to transform himself into a Christ figure, a poet-creator.

Lezama proposes a universe brought about by the Image, a world with which the human subject can have an intimate relationship. Another universe apart from the Image, one that must be perceived as an object held at a distance, lies outside Lezama's vision. However, time always introduces an external factor into the relationship between mind and its own universe. What we experience today will seem tomorrow as something apart from us, something external to us. It is at this point that history assumes its role in the thought of Lezama, a providential and imaginary history that presumes to take into account both time and change within a universe evolving toward the Image of total creativity, where Time no longer exists. Meanwhile, suggests Lezama, the creative power of the Image allows us to transcend the alienation and externalization effected by Time. Historical events take shape by way of the infinite Image realizing itself in the finite world of metaphorical comparison.

For Lezama, history is the reflection of the Image projecting itself through the historical process and through time. The imaginary course of history in Lezama has no particular starting point and is a dynamic and multidimensional process, analogous to the same rich profusion found in baroque writing. The "author" of a text is actually the mediator between two images: a lost past and a future that can never be completely attained at the human level. What exists is a text comprising a precarious status that can only present itself as a possible future or, as Lezama calls it, as "the uncreated" in the process of being created. This is, for Lezama, the baroque writing, which, owing to its basic instability, sustains the flow of the text and the progress of history. As we have noted, this idea opposes Spengler's comparison of homologous forms and his cyclical universe of eternal return in which history unceasingly repeats itself. From Lezama's viewpoint, without the time factor of the metaphorical human subject and the survival of the Image, which gives meaning to each culture, history would be circular or, at best, composed of cycles with neither direction nor consequence. It is within this context that Lezama's subject, as a finite manifestation of the Image, provides the elements of dynamic continuity to history and culture combined.

Carpentier would agree with Lezama about the interplay between nature and the human subject who interprets the historical process, but he would disagree with the religious and "imaginary" position that Lezama attributes to the interchange between the manifestation of the Image and human will.[21] In lieu of the idealistic dialectics of Hegel or the historical-scientific dialectics of Marx, Lezama believes in a history based on the Image that comports itself with the characteristics of fiction.[22] He concurs with Vico in the conception of a history that is neither linear nor circular, but shaped as a spiral spinning itself out in search of a kind of providential salvation. He also agrees with Curtius, who saw in every historical "act" a specific instance of entropy or indeterminacy that, in turn, signifies the very source of creativity.[23]

From Lezama's perspective, to attempt to reconstruct history is to create a kind of fiction that requires constant reinvention. This is a sort of re-creation in which the human subject, in the role of mediator, must take an ethical/aesthetic stance from which to weave the historical narrative. In the Lezamian universe, an act of history can never be reproduced exactly, only re-invented or re-created.[24] To recover the past would imply the ability to return precisely to a point of origin that has since escaped any grasp. The indeterminacy or symbolic ambiguity of any event renders impossible an absolutely precise reproduction of that event and thus allows for creativity. The fictionalization of history involves both a romantic utopia and the impossibility of achieving such a utopia.[25] In this sense Carpentier, particularly in his novels written after 1956, relates the historical process with the essence of narration and reaffirms the fact that this form of development is profoundly revolutionary.[26]

For Lezama, both history and fiction are generated in a baroque way, from a tension between the past and the future that spins around a pivotal vacuum.[27] If history (or for that matter writing) had a specific, defined point of origin, then, once this ideal point was specified, everything would come to a stop. In other words, if Lezama had arrived at *the beginning* in "Paradiso," or if Carpentier had uncovered, in his trip down the Orinoco, the "lost steps," then history would have been "halted" at that point, objectified.

However, the possibility of the return of a lost paradise and the arrival of a kingdom on this earth, even though unobtainable in the strictest sense, implies the necessity of a positive force for the realm of history as much as for that of writing. For Lezama, the important objective is not so much to hit the target as to shoot the arrow. One way or another there will be a reward. Thus the spiraling movement of Spanish American baroque never implies the ineptitude of chaos, but on the contrary is the only direction toward hope and progress.

To develop his progressive conception of Latin American history, Lezama refers frequently to the Roman conquests, contrasting them with the colonization of the Americas. This comparison serves to accentuate the marginal character of his historical human subject. According to Lezama, the Roman world was always expanding yet never lost touch with its central cultural sensibility, its corpus, which imprinted upon the conquered the indisputable style of the conqueror. The Romans were completely convinced of the barbarism of those populations they subjugated, and only those groups who made a concerted effort to retain something of their own customs and values managed to preserve some sense of cultural identity. Yet, despite the immense difficulties, the "barbarian" cultural waves were a constant affirmation of resistance, and at the roots of Hispanic culture we find the conflict between Roman law and Celtic insubordination. This "rebellious Celt" is the metaphorical human subject in the role of cultural resistance that Lezama proposes as the essential thread of historical continuity. These antiauthoritarian movements created sources of imagery that have been enriching our culture since the Middle Ages, images that, despite their apparent chaos, finally found an outlet in the discovery of the Americas. What actually happened was that America became a kind of late Middle Ages. And the fragmentation of medieval Europe was incorporated into the New World. Moreover, "this medievalism has continued as the root of Latin America."[28]

For Lezama, the pre-Renaissance world had a type of imagination that generated a search for a place in which to begin a new culture and re-create its images with innovative myths. This was the quality of imagination that motivated the conquistadors, who found "receptive" American myths already prophesying the arrival of new gods.[29] Whereas in Spain the prose was sophisticated (as seen in that of Cervantes), and the poetry as elaborate as that of Góngora, the chroniclers of the New World managed their primitive narrations with great subtlety in regard to the inventiveness necessary to interpret their new reality. It became their task to sharpen the reaches of the imagination in order to explain the American universe and provide the first European versions of the New World. In effect, they overlay the American landscape with the qualities of creativity found in the novels of chivalry. One becomes immediately aware of this grafting when reading Bernal Díaz del Castillo. This is also true of Oviedo, who related all the new animals of the Americas to those with which he was familiar: lizards became dragons, and bees were compared to flies.[30] The same pattern of narration was employed by the chroniclers of the Indies, at least as far as Lezama was concerned. Their process of interpretation began by enumerating similarities with what they had known in Europe and moved on to descriptions of the differences they perceived in what they saw and touched. For Lezama, the human subject (in this case the European chronicler) functions by means of a metaphorical process that compares the known and the invisible (the image brought over from Europe) with the unknown and the visible (the American landscape). This comparative endeavor gradually creates an image by incorporating and fusing elements from diverse cultures. In this manner the conquistadors and their descendants were able to interpret their adopted world.[31]

It is within this context that Lezama imagines the effect of European influence upon the new American reality, which rises from a culture first determined by the Renaissance and then by the baroque era. Still, there exists for Lezama a fundamental difference between the baroques of Europe and the New World. The European baroque allowed itself to be dictated by the regressive spirit of the Counter-Reformation, whereas its Latin American counterpart aimed at the rebellious spirit of the Counter-Conquest, which opposed European dominance in the New World. Lezama mentions the Indian Kondori as an example of rebellious Latin American baroque. Kondori breaks away from a theological universe closed off by European art in order to integrate elements of Incan culture in his works. We see a similar situation in the case of the mulatto Aleijadinho, who manages to join the elements of Portuguese and African art. In addition, Sor Juana Inés de la Cruz mixes Greek, Christian, and Aztec myths in her play *The Divine Narcissus* (*El Divino Narciso*); in her poem "The Dream" ("El Sueño"), she achieves a poetic level that places Latin American baroque among the stylistic possibilities of high art. Moreover, this early Latin American baroque, which can be traced from the close of the seventeenth century until the close of the eighteenth, was strongly influenced by the Cartesianism and scientism of the Enlightenment. Sor Juana, as well as Carlos Sigüenza y Góngora, exemplifies a baroque art, which prides itself in its scientific precision. Neither in "The Dream" nor in *The Divine Narcissus* does she take recourse in the irrational. To the contrary, everything seems to transpire within a world governed by some type of logic.[32] The kind of baroque that pervades *The Divine Narcissus* would share its affinities more with the "Narcissus" of Valéry than with Lezama's "Death of Narcissus." It is precisely the logical approach to art of the initial Latin American baroque that distinguishes it from the elliptical approach of the contemporary Latin American neobaroque art.

Lezama calls attention to several aspects of the Indian cultures of the Americas. For example, the main character of his novel *Paradiso* is named *Cemí*, which may be derived from *semí*, god of the Taíno Indians. He also establishes a symbolic relationship between the Incan god *Viracocha* and the Aztec *quincunce*. Lezama believes that the element of fertility common to these two mythical elements brings about the fullness of *gnostic space* that generates Latin American culture: "At the heart of Latin American history, at the very center of Incan space, the image continues to win the most decisive battles among the secret pulsations of the invisible toward the image, as anxious to know as to be known."[33] In reference to the African contribution, Lezama gives the example of Aleijadinho. Actually, Lezama's historical and cultural vision assimilates elements from a variety of cultural theories. From the Western traditional view (in this case Hispanic-Lusitanian), he notes the relative importance of the European contribution. Yet despite this, Lezama distances himself from the Western position insofar as it emphasizes the "discovery" as the radical beginning of a new Latin American culture. Furthermore, it would be unthinkable to find in Lezama any agreement with the

Hispanic-Lusitanian idea suggesting that cultural decadence began in Latin America from the moment of its emancipation from Spain and Portugal.[34]

At one point in his writings, Lezama suggests that the arrival of Columbus in America is the foundation of our history: "Our island (Cuba) begins her history within the aegis of poetry. The image, the fable, and the prodigious have been part of our history since the Discovery. Thus, the Admiral Christopher Columbus entered in his *Diary*, a book that stands at the very threshold of our poetry, that, approaching our coasts, he saw a great plume of fire tumble to the sea, an early indication of the seductive power of our light."*[35] This observation may lead the reader to mistakenly conclude that Lezama intends to integrate his view of Latin American culture with that of Eurocentrism, which emphasizes the radical importance of the Hispanic-Lusitanian culture in the history of Latin America. In fact Lezama repeatedly affirms the importance of both Indian and African cultures.

Lezama's *Americanism*, like that of many of the Latin Americans of his generation, is an encompassing theoretical formulation. It aspires to an ontological base for a social reality that in Latin America is perceived as a threat to regional identity. The proponents of Americanism took various orientations: some concentrated on cultural projects, almost always based on ontological and utopian principles, as was the case with most of the members of the "Ateneo de la Juventud" in Mexico; others involved themselves with political reform, such as the followers of the Alianza Popular Revolucionaria Americana (Popular Revolutionary American Alliance), or APRA, in Peru; and still others took part in Socialist programs, as in the case of Mariátegui and other Marxists.[36]

The American Expression, published by Lezama in 1957, includes not only the Americanism and nationalism shared by many Cubans at that time but also some of the Americanist con-

---

* "Nuestra Isla comienza su historia dentro de la poesía. La imagen, la fábula y los prodigios establecen su reino desde nuestra fundamentación y el descubrimiento. Así el almirante Cristóbal Colón consigna en su *Diario*, libro que debe estar en el umbral de nuestra poesía, que vio caer al acercarse a nuestras costas un gran ramo de fuego en el mar. Ya comenzaban las seducciones de nuestra luz."

victions of the members of the "Ateneo de la Juventud," founded in Mexico in 1908. Among the most prominent members of this intellectual group were Antonio Caso, José Vasconcelos, Alfonso Reyes, and the Dominican Pedro Henríquez Ureña. Vasconcelos, in *The Cosmic Race* (*La raza cósmica*) (1926), had conceived a regional integration that carried with it a heightened sense of worth in the Spanish American culture. For Vasconcelos, Spanish America was the space within which the "lost" civilization of Atlantis would become realized. He also believed, along with Lezama, that the destiny of Europe "was to die on foreign shores" owing to a process of desintegration that at the same time fertilized the culture of the Old Continent. It is also important, within this context, to keep in mind *The Boundary* (*El deslinde*) of Alfonso Reyes, published in 1944. In this work, as in his many essays on Americanism, Reyes assumes a humanistic character in order to present a total cultural construct. His work centers on a human subject serving as a pivot around which revolves all the elements that give meaning to that culture. With Reyes's subject we cannot help but be reminded of Lezama's equally fertile metaphorical human subject. With regard to Pedro Henríquez Ureña, his *Six Essays in Search of Our Expression* (*Seis ensayos en busca de nuestra expresión*) (1928) constitutes an invitation to Lezama's future "American expression." The critical humanism of Henríquez Ureña bases his "American expression" in Western civilization. *Six Essays* concerns a cultural reformulation in which the social human subject is transformed and then universalized through the process of *mestizaje*, the mixing of social and cultural values.[37]

In addition to the theories of the "Ateneo" mentioned above, Cuban thought of the late twenties and early thirties was greatly influenced by the *Revista de Avance*, which concerned itself with issues of both national and Latin American identity. Many contributors to this journal developed ideas around this theme in their essays: for example, Jorge Mañach in *An Investigation of Mockery* (*Indagación del choteo*) (1928), and Juan Marinello in *About Cuban Restlessness* (*Sobre la inquietud cubana*) (1930) and *American and Cuban Literary Expressions* (*Americanismos y cubanismos literarios*) (1932). But Lezama has a greater intellectual affinity for the ideas of some of the members of the Mexican "Ateneo" than for those of the majority of his countrymen in the

Revista de Avance, a point clearly demonstrated in his public debate against Jorge Mañach in 1949.[38]

For Lezama, history is an ascending spiral whose continuity is guaranteed by the rebellious metaphorical human subject. This Lezamian subject, as far as Latin America is concerned, first appeared in the eighteenth century as a result of the cultural symbiosis of Latin America and the "decadent" European culture. Lezama also integrates certain elements of America's colonial past, the reevaluation of the American Indian (Amerindian) world, and the vigor of Latin America's national and regional reaffirmation. There exists a cultural Americanism postulated by the nationalist Latin American bourgeoisie that, in its eagerness for autonomy, attempts to reintroduce the contributions of both the colonial era and the indigenous Amerindian world. Cultural Americanism, despite its serious limitations, opened the way for a history of popular culture in Latin America. It was a stance taken as a way of resisting and improving upon the typically liberal interpretations such as that of Sarmiento and the positivists, which generally despise Indian, black, *gaucho,* and peasant cultures. Lezama's theory tries to improve on the liberalism that suggests the erasure of all history prior to the Colonial Independence Movement. This posture not only negates the influence of Spain and Portugal but at the same time would propose the history of European capitalism of the Enlightenment as the only connection with world history. Lezama's stance also differs from the theory of a radical proletarian culture that denies the importance of anything prior to its formation in Latin America.[39]

History for Lezama proceeds by creating a spiral that opens onto the possibility of human progress. This perspective helps explain why he included the Cuban Revolution of 1959 in his view of historical progression. For Lezama, the Cuban Revolution is the last "imaginary era":

The final imaginary era is the era of infinite possibility, which, among us, has been in line with José Martí. Among the more significant meanings of the Cuban Revolution, to stand in opposition to the era of insanity, dissipation, and false riches, is to have brought about again the spirit of radiant poverty, of the poor man with an overabundance drawn from the gifts of the spirit. Our nineteenth century drew creation from its poverty. From the modest glasses of Varela to the frock coat of the solemn speeches of Martí, all our men of substance were poor men. Certainly there were rich men in the nineteenth century who participated in the ascending process of the nation. But they began by giving up their riches, by dying in exile, by giving throughout the extent of their fields a stroke of a bell that called for a return to an essential poverty, losing themselves in the forest, in wonderings, in distant exile, to begin again in the most primordial and naked fashion.... All images now have the height and the force of magic. Everything weaves this possibility, like a spark of energy transfigured in an instant into a seed. The transfigured earth receives this seed and develops it to the utmost of its possibilities. Thus now our peasants are happy because they find themselves within the melody of our destiny.

The Cuban Revolution demonstrates that all the negative spells have been beheaded.... When the People is inhabited by a living image, the State accomplishes its perfect form.*[40]

Lezama considers as equally important the arrival of the Europeans in the New World, the Wars of Independence, and the

---

* "La última era imaginaria, a la cual voy a aludir en esta ocasión, es la posibilidad infinita, que entre nosotros la acompaña José Martí. Entre las mejores cosas de la Revolución cubana, reaccionando contra la era de la locura que fue la etapa de la disipación, de la falsa riqueza, está el haber traído de nuevo el espíritu de la pobreza irradiante, del pobre sobreabundante por los dones del espíritu. El siglo XIX, el nuestro, fue creador desde su pobreza. Desde los espejuelos modestos de Varela, hasta la levita de las oraciones solemnes de Martí, todos nuestros hombres esenciales fueron hombres pobres. Claro que hubo hombres ricos en el siglo XIX, que participaron del proceso ascencional de la nación. Pero comenzaron por quemar sus riquezas, por morirse en el destierro, por dar en toda la extensión de sus campiñas un campanazo que volvía a la pobreza más esencial, a perderse en el bosque, a lo errante, a la lejanía, a comenzar de nuevo en una forma primigenia y desnuda.... Toda imagen tiene ahora el altitudo y la fuerza de su posibilidad. Todos los posibles atraviesan la puerta de los hechizos. Todos los hechizos ovillan esa posibilidad, como una energía que en un instante es un germen. La tierra transfigurada recibe ese germen y lo hincha al extremo de sus posibilidades. Son así ahora alegres nuestros campesinos al estar muy adentro en la melodía de nuestro destino. La Revolución cubana significa que todos los conjuros negativos han sido decapitados.... Cuando el pueblo está habitado por una imagen viviente, el estado alcanza su figura."

Amerindian contributions. Furthermore, the romantic rebellion, for Lezama, was more than a radical break since it "brought to the fore historical circumstance," and the Incan dimension that Bolívar received from his teacher Simón Rodríguez "was the root that made possible the movement toward independence."[41] In the period from the eighteenth to the nineteenth centuries, from baroque to romanticism in Latin America, Lezama traces the Latin American cultural itinerary through a human subject whose rebelliousness and marginality are demonstrated in the exile of Fray Servando Teresa de Mier, the dungeons of Francisco Miranda, the solitude of Simón Rodríguez, and, at the end of the nineteenth century, the tribulations of José Martí, who managed to reconstruct and redefine the image of both Cuba and Latin America.[42]

To sum up, Lezama takes from the Western, Hispanic-Lusitanian cultural theory the relative importance of the colonial past yet strongly rejects the colonial idea of a fall into decadence following the Wars of Independence. From nineteenth-century liberalism, he assimilates the reaffirmation of nationalism but distances himself from the typically liberal disparagement of the Indian, the black, the *gaucho*, and the peasant. From twentieth-century bourgeois Latin Americanism, Lezama accepts the rediscovery not only of the colonial past but also of the Amerindian cultures. Finally, when he integrates the contribution of the Cuban Revolution with his vision, Lezama's historical conception moves toward a perspective far more radical than typical bourgeois Latin Americanism. For Lezama, the Latin American human subject evolves from a rebellious cultural stance that includes many classes, races, and ethnic groups. In different ways and at different times, these groups have set themselves against a dominant social system that stood in the way of the process of cultural affirmation and the subsequent historical progress toward an essential betterment.

Lezama's idea of historical development views the Latin American as taking into his or her possession the fruits of the Old World to revitalize and transcend them. Thus, in order to speak of Lezama's *American Expression* we might call to mind the *Ismaelillo* of Martí. Published in 1882, this volume of poetry is characterized by Martí's use of the poetic voice of a father who has revered his son to the point of making him assume the role of father, while he himself takes on the role of son. In *Ismaelillo*,

Martí expresses the significance of the son as an example of the authentic, of something beyond the norms of nineteenth-century mercantile society. By aggrandizing the son, Martí manages to place in context as well as question the adult values of the times. The child must beware of the "yellow king," the gold that the poet associates with decadence, impurity, and death. The child is an Adam-like figure that expresses "for the first time" the possibilities of the universe. In *Ismaelillo*, as in his other writings and his political activities, Martí promotes an indigenous Latin American culture with which to confront the European influence of the nineteenth century and the dangers of North American expansionism. This opposition is directed not only toward political and economic dominance but also toward the cultural sphere. Martí's *Ismaelillo* appears as an optimistic metaphor in the face of enormous threats to Latin American culture. His young protagonist is a fighter, an "unsettled battler" who announces the possibility of a new form of cultural expression in America. Martí chooses a name out of the Middle East for his young America, as an indication of his refusal to embrace a mercantile civilization that progressively threatens the less developed nations and that stands directly in the path of a genuine "Latin American expression."[43] In this sense, Lezama might be seen as continuing Martí's insistence upon indigenous Latin Americanism.

Lezama places himself within a tradition established by Martí yet no longer within that romantic notion wherein the "I" affirms its authenticity through its identification with "the natural." Lezama never seeks to discover the perfect union of the individual genius and Nature through the dialectics of Love—a method more in keeping with the aesthetics of Martí—but rather emphasizes an all-encompassing poetic vision that transcends the romantic concepts of subject and Nature.[44]

As previously noted, Lezama's *metaphorical human subject* is basically a rebellious and marginal one whose greatest moment is characterized by a kind of liberation. In Lezama's conception of history the metaphorical subject first appears as the "rebellious Celt" opposed to Imperial Roman law. However, the Lezamian subject begins to take on its specifically Latin American characteristics in the "criollo" (Creole) of the eighteenth century, a figure formed from the mixing of elements as diverse as Spanish, Portuguese, Indian, and African. Lezama views the eighteenth century as the beginning of a Latin American consciousness, a historical moment within which monks, teachers, sailors, and ranchers began to acquire the "image" of their cultural situation, the "sense of place" within their identity.

Lezama refers to the first Latin American who dominated his world in a manner entirely different from his European counterpart as "nuestro señor barroco" ("our baroque lord" or "our baroque gentleman"): "This American baroque gentleman, authentically rooted in what is ours, in his farm, sinecure, or comfortable house, within the poverty that sharpens the pleasures of the intelligence, appears when the tumult of the conquest has passed and the landscape has already been parceled out by the colonizer."[45] This "baroque gentleman" is the first to feel like an American, master of his environment, interpreter and mediator of the universe through his culture's vision, born of the myth and landscape of the New World. He arrived as the result of (and, paradoxically, the rebellion against) the ascension of the Enlightenment in Latin America. Lezama presents his Latin American metaphorical subject through such personalities as Fray Servando; the Indian Kondori; the mulatto Aleijadinho; the nun Sor Juana; the liberal Francisco Miranda; Simón Rodríguez, advocate of Incan socialism; and the exile, poet, and revolutionary José Martí. With these figures, Lezama insists that his metaphorical subject arises from various classes, ethnicities, races, groups, and historical moments. The common factor for all of them is rebellion, marginality, and a sense of redemption from their specific circumstances of domination. Thus Lezama's subject is presented in opposition to the dominant culture. Yet this rebellion, or marginality, is very different from anarchy. It is directed toward a basically Christian sense of history and toward the poetic interpretation of history. The metaphorical subject is the key element of cultural and historical continuity, particularly as that aspect that interprets the image of the American space (Lezama calls it "gnostic American space") as the realm of future cultural possibility.

The idea of an "American baroque gentleman" seems to have found concrete expression in the character of Amo in Carpentier's *Baroque Concert (Concierto barroco)*.[46] Amo leaves Mexico for Europe, and while passing through Cuba, his servant dies, victim of an epidemic in Havana. Amo needs another servant and employs a black Cuban named Filomeno, the great-grandson of a certain Salvador. According to Silvestre de Balboa's *Mirror of Patience* (*Espejo de paciencia*), this Salvador had helped the Spanish defeat the English pirate Gilbert Giron, who had attacked Manzanillo in the eighteenth century. Here Carpentier merges his narrative with that of Balboa and has Amo continue with Filomeno to Madrid. There Amo is totally disillusioned. The grand city that had been so esteemed from afar is actually a disappointment. This son of the conquistadors is disenchanted with the decadence of Madrid as compared with his native Mexico. Here Carpentier emphasizes not only a Spenglerian decadence but also the reaction of the "American baroque gentleman" (Carpentier would call him "criollo" or Creole) who now has his own sense of pride and rejects the European version of the Conquest. In one of the passages of *Baroque Concert* in which Amo and Filomeno have left Madrid for Italy, Carpentier portrays the indignation of the Mexican at a Vivaldi libretto involving a ridiculous and mistaken view of the relationship between Moctezuma and Cortés. Again disillusioned, Amo decides to return home because he has reassessed of his priorities while watching a European piece about the Americas (in this case Mexico): "And I understood, suddenly, that I counted myself among the Americans."[47] Then this Creole, this "American baroque gentleman," recognizes and voices the credo of the enlightened exile: "At times it is necessary to distance yourself from things ... in order to see things closely."[48] Filomeno, however, has no desire to return to America. He would rather go to Paris where they will call him "Monsieur Philomène"and not "el negrito Filomeno" ("the little black Filomeno").[49] One can infer from the conversations between Amo and Filomeno that Amo is the "American baroque gentleman" of the eighteenth century and Filomeno is the precursor of the runaway, black rebel of the nineteenth century. Filomeno's great-grandfather fought with Spain against the English pirate, but now Filomeno must prepare himself to fight against the Spanish slaveowner. In the nineteenth century Filomeno will join with Amo in the Wars of Independence against the Spanish army.

Within Lezama's system, there exists in Cuban history a kind of "baroque gentleman of Independence" exemplified by Carlos Manuel de Céspedes. Even though the "Latin American baroque gentleman" evolves in the eighteenth century as a reaction to the

Enlightenment, Lezama seems to suggest that Céspedes is, in a certain manner, the Cuban figure who most exemplifies the characteristics of the "baroque gentleman," despite his being a liberator with close ties to the romantic rebellion of the Independence Movement. Céspedes is the hero of the initial moment in 1868 of Cuba's "Ten-years War," at which time he freed his slaves, thus beginning the first War of Independence in Cuba. Lezama, in an essay entitled "Céspedes: The Founding Majesty" ("Céspedes: el señorío fundador"), says: "His sense of eminence, though still challenged by the magisterial traditions of Spain, led him to decide to enter Bayamo beneath crossed swords. Though the test is perfect and the style beyond reproach, he grasps with typical quickness that he is under the obligation to begin a new tradition, in which all is festive, all a luxury of friendship ... an eminence in rebellion that seeks fresh blood and a new mystery."*[50] Through the figure of Céspedes, Lezama introduces what we might call *the myth of the hero entering the city*.[51] Thus the death of Céspedes is especially important within the Cuban mythos: "the sound of gunshots. Dragged behind a horse, he enters Santiago. And in this way he belongs to those who have entered into the promised city dead." The death of Céspedes, and of the other Cuban heroes who have been unable to enter the "promised city" (Santiago de Cuba) alive, is like a mythical force that submerges itself in order to reappear later with more vigor: "the land, which returns that which it destroys, changes the dead hero into those legions that climb toward the stars in order to take possession of the new challenges of fire."†[52]

As expected, the figure of José Martí plays the central role in the Cuban mythology created by Lezama. Martí not only initiates great literary and linguistic changes but also contributes importantly to the construction of both Cuban and Latin American affirmation. For Lezama, Martí voices a literary revolution whose

---

* "Su señorío, aun presionado por la majestad a la española, decide entrar bajo palio en Bayamo. Aunque la prueba es cabal y el estilo queda a salvo, comprende con rapidez nuestra que está en la obligación de inaugurar una nueva tradición, donde todo es como una fiesta, un lujo de la amistad ... el señorío que se rebela y busca otra sangre y un nuevo misterio."

† "la tierra, que devuelve lo que devora, convierte al héroe muerto en legión alegre que trepa por lo estelar, para apoderarse del nuevo reto del fuego."

ends will be realized in the course of history: with him, "poetry becomes a choral song." Lezama refers to Martí as "a fertile god, an engenderer of the Cuban image. He arrived by means of the image to create a reality, and at our very foundations lies this image as the support that sustains the counterpoint of our people."[*][53]

The death of Martí also becomes a fundamental part of *the myth of the hero entering the city*: "We see how he has been dragged through the rain after his death, how fainting from his steed he prompted the few who saw it to remark that perhaps he had groaned, how he has been buried and unburied ..., his head separated from his trunk, as in those shrieking displays of the Mongolian cavalry, staged before the gates of the city."[†][54]

The city is Cuba's Santiago, a metaphor that serves as support for the image of the rebel hero who, as long as he remains in the forest or mountains, cannot become part of the history of his people. From this point of view, the city is the metaphor within which the image of the hero is contained and developed, and thus it is within the city that the aspirations of the hero can be fulfilled. Otherwise, history would remain only as a possibility, since the image of the hero in the forest could not be realized in the urban metaphor. It is also interesting to note that although Havana is the "space" within which Cemí realizes himself as poet in *Paradiso*, it is Santiago, one of the main centers of revolution in Cuba, that appears as the promised city of Lezama's rebellious hero. Since urban space is the historical metaphor of the possibilities of the Image in this specific mythology, it is of utmost importance whether the hero enters the city alive or dead. It is within this context that Lezama associates the figure of Martí with the Cuban Revolution of 1959: "But Martí touched the earth and kissed it and created a new causality, as all the great poets do. This was the prelude to a poetic era among us; so that we can now

---

[*] "siendo un dios fecundante, un preñador de la imagen de lo cubano. Llegó la imagen a crear una realidad, en nuestra fundamentación está esa imagen como sustentáculo del contrapunto de nuestro pueblo."

[†] "Vemos cómo ha sido arrastrado después de muerto bajo la lluvia, cómo al desplomarse del alazán algunos que lo vieron dicen que aún gemía, cómo ha sido enterrado y desenterrado ... cómo su cabeza separada del tronco, como en los alardes chillantes de una caballería mongólica, ha sido mostrada a la entrada de la ciudad."

begin to live in an era that is infinitely affirmative, central, creative. It is the discovery of the ring, of the absolute circle. The hero enters the city."*55

In summary, for Lezama, to live is to re-create. However, this kind of re-creation involves an evolution that always permits the possibilities of the future. In this way, Lezama's history functions in the same way as the narrative process, as a kind of *dramatis personae* in progression, an unfolding that develops from a fragmented reality. The fragmentation is an error that is based on the Image, which, in turn, is the reality of reality. Thus the poetry of Lezama insists that the quest of the romantic subject for complete fulfillment of the self is not possible at the purely human level, yet there is no cause to refrain from aspiring for this complete fulfillment. This search becomes more urgent in times of crisis, especially since it is a desire to respond to the anxiety produced by a hostile social context, by a society that has lost its sense of orientation. The fragmentation of reality results in a polarization of social and cultural forces, and it is here that the Lezamian Image opens itself to the possibility of embracing the vacuum between these polarities. Since a society in crisis alienates the person from his or her environment and emphasizes irony as the mode of dominant discourse, the person has no choice but to create a marginal reaction that tends toward the imagination. With the separation of human consciousness and the social world, a situation that characterizes industrial society, it becomes necessary "to create" in order to give some sense of meaning to cultural mutations. In Lezama's system, the Image is the source of all reality; it is the "substance of the real." All is created and re-created continually as the Image progresses in a metaphorical process that strings together the most diverse of elements and unites at an imaginary level all that appears fragmentary.

It can be said that for Lezama the purely "American being" does not exist. More precisely, it does not exist so much as a pure being but more as fragments woven together, a being without a privileged, logocentric place of origin. Lezama sees the "American

---

* "Pero Martí tocó la tierra, la besó, creó una nueva causalidad, como todos los grandes poetas. Y fue el preludio de la era poética entre nosotros, que ahora nuestro pueblo comienza a vivir, era inmensamente afirmativa, cenital, creadora. Encuentro del anillo, del círculo absoluto. El héroe entra en la ciudad."

being" as something more along the lines of a quilt woven by a metaphorical subject with the scraps and pieces of various cultures. This vision of Latin American culture, with its complexity and richness, stands at the very heart of Lezama's poetics. Thus within Lezama's conception of poetry there exists a rhapsody sung from the vacuum created by an absent Nature as well as a subject entwined in metaphorical language that arises from the ashes of decline. Finally, Latin America expresses its "American being" as a tissue stretched across the space created by the lack of an "American origin." The "American being" is constructed in a historical unfolding that progresses toward the reinvention of a subject and a society in crisis.

Notes

Introduction

1. José Lezama Lima, "X y XX," in *Obras completas*, 2:146.
2. Lezama Lima, "Mitos y cansancio clásico," in *Obras completas*, 2:279.
3. Although my text, *La subversión de la semiótica*, coauthored with Professor Ramiro Fernández, was not published until 1988, it is, for the most part, a result of our interests and studies during the 1970s. Its primary concern is to present a critical history of Western European structuralism beginning with Saussure. However, our last chapter considers two critical perspectives, which are "poststructuralist": Derrida's "deconstruction" and the "neo-Marxism" of Fredric Jameson. Thus our book treats not only a subversion caused *by* structuralist semiotics but also the subversion *of* semiotics by other critical perspectives. See Emilio Bejel and Ramiro Fernández, *La subversión de la semiótica. Análisis estructural de textos hispánicos.*
4. Lezama Lima, "Obra póstuma de Nietzsche," in *Obras completas*, 2:575–78.
5. Martin Heidegger, "Nietzsche as Metaphysician."
6. I am aware of the controversy regarding the terms *modernity* and *postmodernity*. I prefer, however, not to enter into this debate at present but simply to define the "postmodern" as a project beginning at the margins of rational metaphysics that privileges poetic discourse over logical or conceptual discourse.
7. Lezama Lima, "Nuevo Mallarmé II," in *Obras completas*, 2:529.
8. Lezama Lima, "El 26 de julio: imagen y posibilidad," in *Imagen y posibilidad*, introduction and selection by Ciro Bianchi Ross, pp. 19–22.
9. See the comments on this topic made by Cintio Vitier in an interview with me published in *Areíto* 27 (1981):30–34.
10. See, for example, the following: Efraín Barradas, "La revista *Orígenes* (1944–1956)"; Graciela García Marruz, "La obra poética de Cintio Vitier"; Alessandra Riccio, "Los años de *Orígenes*"; and José Prats Sariol, "La revista *Orígenes*."
11. Some of the most recent articles on this topic can be found in *Coloquio*, vol. 1. This and a second volume are collections of the lectures and presentations from the symposium on Lezama Lima and his work held at the University of Poitiers in 1982.
12. Some of the articles that deal directly with this debate include the following: Armando Álvarez Bravo, "La novela de Lezama Lima"; Cintio Vitier and Fina García Marruz, "Respuesta a Armando Álvarez Bravo";

Manuel Pereira, "José Lezama Lima: las cartas sobre la mesa"; Enrico Mario Santí, "La invención de Lezama Lima"; Emilio Bejel, "Entrevista con Cintio Vitier"; Lisandro Otero, "Para una definición mejor de Lezama Lima"; Armando Hart Dávalos, "Entrevista"; Manuel Moreno Fraginals, "Lezama Lima y la Revolución"; Gustavo Pellón, "Portrait of the Cuban Writer as French Painter: Henri Rousseau, José Lezama Lima's Alter Ego."

13. See the comments made by Cintio Vitier in his interview with me in *Areíto*.

14. Cintio Vitier explains this incident in the interview in *Areíto*. One of the strongest attacks against Lezama, Vitier, and the "*Orígenes* group" was made by Heberto Padilla in "La poesía en su lugar." Also see the comments on this issue made by Guillermo Cabrera Infante, former director of *Lunes de Revolución* who has lived in London for many years, in "Encuentros y recuerdos con José Lezama Lima."

15. See Cabrera Infante, "Encuentros y recuerdos con José Lezama Lima.

16. One of the most detailed accounts of this incident is found in Pellón, "Portrait of the Cuban Writer as French Painter." Pellón correctly emphasizes the very important role played by the Argentine writer Julio Cortázar in the publication, defense, and dissemination of *Paradiso*.

17. See Lourdes Casal, *El caso Padilla*. For an analysis and bibliography on this "affair," see Charles Hollingsworth, "The Development of Literary Theory in Cuba, 1959–1968." See also Padilla's own account of this incident in relation to Lezama, in Heberto Padilla, "Lezama Lima frente a su discurso."

18. See Vitier's interview in *Areíto*.

19. See Eloísa Lezama Lima's publication of her brother's letters, *Cartas (1939–1976)*. Some critics have questioned Eloísa Lezama Lima's selection of her brother's correspondence; see especially Pereira, "José Lezama Lima" as well as Cintio Vitier, "De las cartas que me escribió Lezama."

20. See Armando Álvarez Bravo's debate on this issue, "La novela de Lezama Lima"; and see Cintio Vitier and Fina García Marruz, "Respuesta a Armando Álvarez Bravo."

Chapter 1. Rhapsody for an Absent Nature

1. José Lezama Lima, "Respuesta y nuevas interrogaciones. Carta abierta a Jorge Mañach."

2. Ibid.

3. See Aristotle, *On the Art of Poetry*.

4. Ibid.

5. See Giambattista Vico, *The New Science*.

6. See Percy B. Shelley, *A Defense of Poetry*.

7. See John Moran, ed. and trans., *Rousseau—Herder: On the Origin of Language*, pp. 87–176. See also a study of the relationship between Herder and Vico in Isaiah Berlin, *Vico and Herder*.

8. See Samuel Taylor Coleridge, *Biographia Literaria;* and John Spencer Hill, ed., *Imagination in Coleridge.*
9. See M. H. Abrams, *Natural Supernaturalism. Tradition and Revolution in Romantic Literature.*
10. See Oscar Rivera-Rodas, "Teoría hispanoamericana de la poesía: 1823–1920," pp. 29–52. See also Pedro Grases, in the Prologue to Andrés Bello, *Antología de Andrés Bello.*
11. See the contrast drawn between Bello and Heredia by Rivera–Rodas, "Teoría hispanoamericana de la poesía," pp. 29-52.
12. Ibid.
13. Octavio Paz, *Los hijos del limo,* esp. pp. 48–60.
14. See Salvador Arias, "Nuestro primer gran poema. (Estudio de 'En el Teocalli de Cholula' de José María Heredia.)"
15. See José Carlos Ballón, "Autonomía cultural: de Emerson a Martí," pp. 62–94. For a study of the metaphor of the "Yellow King," which refers to the impurity of gold, see Ivan Schulman, *Símbolo y color en la obra de José Martí,* pp. 409–11. Martí expresses his ideas on Nature and the Self in relation to those of Emerson's in "Emerson."
16. See J. H. Van den Berg, "The Subject and His Landscape," p. 57.
17. Giuseppe Mazzotta, *Dante, Poet of the Desert,* esp. pp. 227–74.
18. See Rubén Ríos-Ávila, "A Theology of Absence: The Poetic System of José Lezama Lima," pp. 63–76.
19. Lezama Lima, "Rapsodia para el mulo," in *Obras completas,* 1:824–28.
20. Lezama Lima, "Confluencias," in *Obras completas,* 2:1212–13.

Chapter 2. Narcissus in the Language of Cassandra

1. For a general study of the historical evolution of these ideas, see Karl D. Uitti, *Linguistics and Literary Theory,* esp. pp. 38–62. For a penetrating analysis of the relationship between history and rhetoric in Dante, see Giuseppe Mazzotta, *Dante, Poet of the Desert,* esp. pp. 227–74. For a study of Dante's concept of language, see André Pézard, "La langue italienne dans la pensée de Dante."
2. For an interesting interpretation of the idea of postmodernity in Nietzsche, Heidegger, and Derrida, see Richard E. Palmer, "The Postmodernity of Heidegger"; Joseph N. Riddle, "From Heidegger to Derrida to Chance: Doubling and (Poetic) Language"; and Frances C. Ferguson, "Reading Heidegger: Paul DeMan and Jacques Derrida."
3. Martin Heidegger, "Nietzsche as Metaphysician."
4. Lezama Lima, "Introducción a un sistema poético," in *Obras completas,* 2:425–27.
5. Ibid., pp. 425–27.
6. José Lezama Lima, "La imagen histórica," in *Obras completas,* 2:846–48. See also Donald Phillip Verene, *Vico's Science of Imagination,* and Renate Wiesner Holub, "Problematics of Giambattista Vico's Theory of Poetics and Aesthetics."

7. Lezama Lima, "X y XX," in *Obras completas*, 2:146.
8. See Holub, "Problematics of Giambattista Vico's Theory of Poetics and Aesthetics."
9. Lezama Lima, "La biblioteca como dragón," in *Obras completas*, 2:890–925.
10. Lezama Lima, "Los egipcios," in *Obras completas*, 2:873.
11. Ibid., p. 874.
12. Lezama Lima, "Exámenes," in *Obras completas*, 2:214–15.
13. Lezama Lima, "Preludio a las eras imaginarias," in *Obras completas*, 2:809.
14. On Heidegger's concept of *aletheia*, see David Couzens Hoy, "The Owl and the Poet: Heidegger's Critique of Hegel," p. 62.
15. Lezama Lima, "Mitos y cansancio clásico," in *Obras completas*, 2:286.
16. Lezama Lima, "Obra póstuma de Nietzsche," in *Obras completas*, 2:575–78.
17. Lezama Lima, "Muerte de Narciso," in *Obras completas*, 1:653–58. All subsequent quotes will be taken from this edition.
18. Lezama Lima, "La posibilidad del espacio gnóstico americano," in *Imagen y posibilidad*, p. 102.
19. Ibid.
20. Ibid.
21. Lezama Lima, "Preludio a las eras imaginarias," in *Obras completas*, 2:819–20. Also see Lezama's comments on this matter in an interview in Armando Álvarez Bravo, *Órbita de Lezama Lima*, p. 35.
22. See Gérard Genette, "Complejo de Narciso."
23. See Gérard Genette, "Valéry and the Poetics of Language."
24. Ibid., pp. 38–44.
25. See Paul Valéry, *Oeuvres*, 1:1333. Also see Ernest Curtius, *Marcel Proust y Paul Valéry*.
26. Lezama Lima, "El acto poético y Valéry," in *Obras completas*, 2:250–52.
27. Ibid.
28. See Curtius, *Marcel Proust y Paul Valéry*.
29. It is in "Narcisse Parle" in *Album de Vers Anciens*, where Valéry deals with the Narcissus theme for the first time. This theme is not fully developed by Valéry until the publication of his "Fragments du Narcisse" (included in *Charmes*).
30. See Mazotta, *Dante, Poet of the Desert*.
31. Ibid., pp. 60–65.
32. Lezama Lima, "Introducción a un sistema poético," p. 393.
33. Ibid., pp. 393–94.
34. See Louise Vinge, *The Narcissus Theme in Western European Literature up to the Early Nineteenth Century*, pp. 29–33. In relation to Philostratus, Vinge quotes from the English translation by Arthur Fairbanks of Philostratus's *Imagines*.
35. Lezama Lima, "Muerte de Narciso," in *Obras completas*, 1:653.
36. See Vinge, *The Narcissus Theme*, pp. 189–90. Also see Mario Praz,

Studies in Seventeenth-Century Imagery.
37. Vinge, *The Narcissus Theme*, p. 190.
38. Sor Juana Inés de la Cruz, *El divino Narciso*, in *Obras selectas*, pp. 128–91.
39. Lezama Lima, "La curiosidad barroca," in *Obras completas*, 2:313–17.
40. Lezama Lima, "Preludio a las eras imaginarias," ibid., pp. 807–8.
41. Lezama Lima, "Exámenes," ibid., p. 224.

Chapter 3. Salvation through Writing

1. Lezama Lima, "Exámenes," in *Obras completas*, 2:218–19.
2. Lezama Lima, "Llamado del deseoso," in *Obras completas*, 1:759.
3. Lezama Lima, "El puerto," in *Obras completas*, 1:757.
4. Lezama Lima, "El guardián inicia el combate circular," in *Obras completas*, 1:782–86.
5. Lezama Lima, "La esposa en la balanza," in *Obras completas*, 1:761.
6. Lezama Lima, "Encuentro con el falso," in *Obras completas*, 1:763–64.
7. See Jacques Lacan, *Écrits*.
8. Lezama Lima, "El retrato ovalado," in *Obras completas*, 1:777–78.
9. Lezama Lima, "El guardián inicia el combate circular," in *Obras completas*, 1:782–86.
10. Lezama Lima, *Paradiso*, 3d ed., 1973. All quotes are taken from this edition, with the relevant page numbers cited in the text of this chapter.
11. See Paul Jay, *Being in the Text*.
12. See Rubén Ríos-Ávila, "A Theology of Absence: The Poetic System of José Lezama Lima," pp. 130–72.
13. Jay, *Being in the Text*.
14. Ibid., pp. 39–91.
15. For information about the relationships between the characters of *Paradiso* and the family and friends of José Lezama Lima, see Eloísa Lezama Lima, "*Paradiso*: novela poema," in the Introduction to José Lezama Lima, *Paradiso*, ed. Eloísa Lezama Lima, pp. 47–94. The reference to Mamita is on p. 80.
16. Eloísa Lezama Lima, "*Paradiso*: novela poema," p. 83.
17. On this idea, see Ríos-Ávila, "A Theology of Absence," pp. 130–72.
18. Ibid.
19. Most personal friends of Lezama are convinced that he was a homosexual. If this is true, Lezama symbolically used personal characteristics like his asthma and his homosexuality as integral parts of his poetic system.
20. See Ríos-Ávila, "A Theology of Absence," pp. 130–72.
21. Ibid.
22. On this idea of the Platonic dialogues in *Paradiso*, see Ríos-Ávila "A Theology of Absence."
23. John Boswell, *Christianity, Social Tolerance, and Homosexuality.*
24. See Armando Álvarez Bravo, "Órbita de Lezama Lima," in *Órbita de Lezama Lima*, p. 16.

25. See Lezama Lima, "Lectura," in *Imagen y posibilidad,* p. 94.
26. Ibid., pp. 96–97.
27. For the possible relationship between *Paradiso* and the *Bildungsroman,* see Arnaldo Cruz, "*Paradiso* de José Lezama Lima: una problemática de los orígenes," pp. 176–97.
28. Lezama Lima, "Nuevo Mallarmé II," in *Obras completas,* 2:529.
29. Here Ríos-Ávila follows Georges Poulet, *The Interior Distance,* p. 240.
30. See Ríos-Ávila, "A Theology of Absence," p. 34.
31. Ibid., p. 20.
32. Ibid., pp. 34–35. See also J. P. Richard, *L'univers imaginaire de Mallarmé,* p. 373.
33. Richard, *L'univers imaginaire,* p. 373.
34. For a comparison between Lezama and Góngora, see Roberto González Echevarría, "Apetitos de Góngora y Lezama."
35. Jay, *Being in the Text,* pp. 92–114.
36. Lezama Lima, "Preludio a las eras imaginarias," in *Obras completas,* 2:819–20. See also Álvarez Bravo, *Órbita de Lezama Lima,* p. 35.

Chapter 4. Poetry after the Storm

1. In 1977, the year after José Lezama Lima's death, two editions of his unfinished manuscript titled *Oppiano Licario* were published, one in Mexico and one in Havana. All quotes are taken from the Mexican edition, with the relevant page numbers cited in the text of this chapter. In addition to the two editions, there is an outline of the unfinished narration of *Oppiano Licario* left by Lezama. In May 1988, in a visit to Cuba, I was able to acquire a copy of this outline thanks to the Cuban writers César López and Abel Prieto. Nevertheless, Professor Enrico Mario Santí obtained a copy of the same outline some years earlier, and in 1984 he published an article about *Oppiano Licario,* taking into account Lezama's outline of the novel. See note 3 below.
2. Several critics have agreed that this particular text not only complements *Paradiso* but is its continuation. For that matter, Lezama's intention to write a continuation and possible clarification of his *Paradiso* is documented in a number of letters to his sister Eloísa Lezama Lima in 1966, as well as those to the sculptor Alfredo Lozano. See José Lezama Lima, *Cartas (1939–1976),* pp. 117, 172, 196.
3. For the analysis of this technique in Lezama, see Enrico Mario Santí's "*Oppiano Licario,* la poética del fragmento."
4. For a study of the *tokonoma* in the poetic system of Lezama, see the interesting article of Leonor Álvarez de Ulloa, "Ordenamiento secreto de la poética de Lezama."
5. For a study of the relationship between Lezama's poetics and Henry Rousseau's art, see Ríos-Ávila, "A Theology of Absence," and Gustavo Pellón, "Portrait of the Cuban Writer as French Painter."
6. See Santí, "*Oppiano Licario,* la poética del fragmento."
7. The complete Spanish title of Licario's manuscript is *Súmula, nunca*

infusa, de excepciones morfológicas.
8. Reynaldo González, "Entre la magia y la infinitud."
9. Lezama Lima, "Esbozo para el *Inferno,*"p. 5 (unpublished).

Chapter 5. The New Shores of Taurus

1. Several Cuban and Latin American authors of this generation read Spengler and other German thinkers through the translations of *Revista de occidente,* founded and directed by José Ortega y Gasset (see José Antonio Portuondo, *Bosquejo histórico de las letras cubanas*). In this chapter I have used Oswald Spengler's *The Decline of the West,* trans. Charles Francis Atkinson. Ideas similar to those expressed in this chapter appear in my article "Cultura y Filosofía de la Historia (Spengler, Carpentier, Lezama Lima)."
2. Alejo Carpentier, "La ciudad de las columnas," and "Lo barroco y lo real maravilloso," pp. 61, 64.
3. José Lezama Lima, "Las imágenes posibles," in *Obras completas,* 2:182.
4. Ibid., pp. 181–82.
5. Lezama emphasizes the relationship between landscape and culture in several of his works, especially in "Mitos y cansancio clásico," in *La expresión americana,* pp. 9–14, 27. For Lezama, this relationship implies a certain kind of spontaneity or vitalism that is the opposite of Hegel's self-awareness as the objective of historical progress. On this point, as on many others, Hegel and Spengler are opposed to each other. Both agree, nevertheless, on a conception of history as a movement (in Spengler cyclical and in Hegel dialectical) of fragmentation and restoration, of fall and redemption. Carpentier and Lezama, each in his own way, share the belief in this dynamic movement of history.
6. For a critical view on Spengler, see R. G. Collingwood, "Oswald Spengler and the Theory of Historical Cycles."
7. Carpentier, "Lo barroco y lo real maravilloso," pp. 61, 64, 69.
8. See Roberto González Echevarría, *Alejo Carpentier: The Pilgrim at Home,* pp. 41–42, 259.
9. See Carpentier, "Lo barroco y lo real maravilloso," pp. 51–73.
10. Lezama Lima, "La curiosidad barroca," in *La expresión americana,* pp. 45–81.
11. Lezama criticizes Worringer's dislike for baroque art. Nevertheless, some similarities exist between Lezama's opinion on baroque art and Worringer's opinion on Gothic art. See Wilhelm Worringer, *Form in Gothic.*
12. In his essay "El papel social del novelista," Carpentier seems to deny individual or historical religious transcendence. Lezama's "religiosity" often assimilates pagan concepts like those of being, subject, and so on.
13. Several of Carpentier's novels deal with topics that take place at the end of the eighteenth century or the beginning of the nineteenth century. Such an insistence suggests that Carpentier places the birth of Cuban culture at that time in history. Other historians prefer to label the begin-

ning of the Cuban War for Independence in 1868 as the birth of a collective revolutionary consciousness in that country. This has been a very controversial topic not only regarding the dates of such a cultural beginning but also concerning the methodology used to arrive at any conclusions.

14. Lezama Lima, "Mitos y cansancio clásico," pp. 14–16.

15. Ibid., pp. 9–11.

16. The metaphorical process that relates a visible form with an invisible one is actually an elliptical process. For an interesting study of the ellipsis in baroque and neobaroque art, see Severo Sarduy, *Barroco.*

17. Lezama Lima, "Mitos y cansancio clásico,"pp. 20–21, 26.

18. González Echevarría has noted the relationship between the ideas of Vico and those of Carpentier. See González Echevarría, *Alejo Carpentier: The Pilgrim at Home,* p. 259.

19. The anti-Cartesian position of Vico is well established. Concerning Carpentier, it can be noted that the title of his novel, *El recurso del método,* is used ironically in reference to Descartes's *El discurso del método.* Regarding Lezama, it would not be an exaggeration to say his entire work is based on an anti-Cartesian concept of knowledge. See Lezama's commentaries on Vico in "A partir de la poesía," in *Obras completas,* 2:831–32.

20. See Verene, *Vico's Science of Imagination,* and also Holub, "Problematics of Giambattista Vico's Theory of Poetics and Aesthetics."

21. Lezama's concept of the Image seems to imply a religious *telos.* On the contrary, Carpentier often bases his opinions on the idea of *context* (in the Sartrean sense of the term).

22. Lezama Lima, "Mitos y cansancio clásico," p. 18.

23. See my article "Lezama o las equiprobabilidades del olvido."

24. Lezama Lima, "Mitos y cansancio clásico."

25. On the theme of the romantic utopia, see Abrams, *Natural Supernaturalism.*

26. Carpentier's novels repeatedly insist on the necessity of radical historical changes, with revolutions.

27. González Echevarría develops this idea regarding Carpentier, especially in the last chapter of his book about the Cuban novelist. See González Echevarría, *Alejo Carpentier: The Pilgrim at Home,* pp. 213–74.

28. Lezama Lima, "Imagen de América Latina."

29. Lezama Lima, "Mitos y cansancio clásico," p. 33.

30. Lezama Lima, "Imagen de América Latina," p. 464.

31. Lezama Lima, "La curiosidad barroca," p. 48.

32. See my article "El sujeto metafórico en Lezama Lima, Valéry y Sor Juana."

33. Lezama Lima, "Imagen de América Latina," p. 468.

34. For an interesting discussion of the relationships between literature, culture, and political orientations in Spanish America during the 1910–40 period, see Mabel Moraña, "Literatura y cultura nacional en Hispanoamérica (1910–1940)."

35. Lezama Lima, "Prólogo a la poesía cubana," in *La cantidad hechizada*, p. 83.

36. Ibid., p. 83.

37. Among the extensive bibliography dealing with the "Ateneo de la Juventud," the following items are directly related to the topic in question here: Soledad Álvarez, "Sobre el americanismo de Pedro Henríquez Ureña"; José Luis Martínez, "La obra de Alfonso Reye"; and Edmundo O'Gorman, "Teoría del deslinde y deslinde de la Teoría."

38. See chapter 1, above.

39. See Moraña, "Literatura y cultura nacional."

40. Lezama Lima, "A partir de la poesía," in *Obras completas*, 2:838–40.

41. Lezama Lima, "Imagen de América Latina," p. 468.

42. The idea of alienation or marginality in Lezama is based on a mythical conception related to an "original lack" that separated Man from the Divine. See Lezama Lima, "La curiosidad barroca" and "El romanticismo y el hecho americano," pp. 45–117.

43. Ballón, "Autonomía cultural," pp. 62–94.

44. Ibid.

45. Lezama Lima, "La curiosidad barroca," p. 48.

46. This idea of the relationship between Lezama's "baroque gentleman" and Amo in Carpentier's *Baroque Concert* was suggested to me by Roberto González Echevarría.

47. Carpentier, *Concierto barroco*, pp. 67–68.

48. This concept can be contrasted with Bertolt Brecht's *Verfremdung*.

49. Carpentier, *Concierto barroco*, p. 79.

50. Lezama Lima, "Céspedes: el señorío fundador," in *Imagen y posibilidad*, p. 25.

51. Some years ago, I believe in 1979, I attended a lecture by Cintio Vitier where he presented the idea of "the myth of the hero entering the city" in Lezama's work. I have not been able to find the publication of this lecture.

52. Lezama Lima, "El 26 de julio: imagen y posibilidad," in *Imagen y posibilidad*, p. 21.

53. Ibid.

54. Lezama Lima, "La posibilidad en el espacio gnóstico americano," in ibid., p. 104.

55. Ibid., pp. 103–4.

Bibliography

The bibliography comprises works consulted in the preparation of this book. For a comprehensive bibliography of works on Lezama Lima, see Justo Ulloa, *Sobre José Lezama Lima y sus lectores: guía y compendio bibliográfico* (Boulder: Society of Spanish and Spanish-American Studies, 1987).

1. Works of Lezama Lima

Cartas (1939–1976). Edited by Eloísa Lezama Lima. Madrid: Editorial Orígenes, 1979.

"Esbozo para el *Infierno*." Unpublished.

Fragmentos a su imán. Havana: Editorial Arte y Literatura, 1977.

Fragmentos a su imán. Mexico: Ediciones Era, 1978.

"Imagen de América Latina." In *América Latina en su literatura*, 4th ed., edited by César Fernández Moreno, 462–68. Mexico: Siglo XXI, 1977.

Imagen y posibilidad. Edited by Ciro Bianchi Ross. Havana: Editorial Letras Cubanas, 1981.

La cantidad hechizada. Havana: UNEAC, 1970.

La cantidad hechizada. Madrid: Ediciones Júcar, 1974.

La expresión americana. Havana: Instituto Nacional de Cultura, Ministerio de Educación, 1957.

La expresión americana. Madrid: Alianza Editorial, 1969.

Obras completas, vol. 1. Mexico: Aguilar, 1975.

Obras completas, vol. 2. Mexico: Aguilar, 1977.

Oppiano Licario. Havana: Editorial Arte y Literatura, 1977.

Oppiano Licario. Mexico: Ediciones Era, 1977; 2d ed., 1978.

Orígenes (Literary magazine, Havana, 1944–56).

Paradiso. Havana: UNEAC, 1966.

Paradiso, 4th ed. Buenos Aires: Ediciones de la Flor, 1972.

Paradiso, 3d ed. Mexico: Ediciones Era, 1973.

Paradiso. Edited by Eloísa Lezama Lima. Madrid: Cátedra, 1980.

Poesía completa. Havana: Instituto del Libro, 1970.

"Respuesta y nuevas interrogaciones. Carta abierta a Jorge Mañach." *Bohemia* 40 (October 2, 1949):77.

2. Criticism on Lezama Lima and Other Works

Abrams, M. H. *Natural Supernaturalism. Tradition and Revolution in Romantic Literature*. New York/London: W. W. Norton, 1973.

Álvarez, Soledad. "Sobre el americanismo de Pedro Henríquez Ureña." *Casa de las Américas* 126 (May-June 1981):63–77.

Álvarez Bravo, Armando. *Lezama Lima: los grandes todos*. Montevideo: ARCA Editorial, 1968.

———. "La novela de Lezama Lima." In *Coloquio internacional* ... 1:87–97. (See *Coloquio internacional* for full reference.)

———. *Órbita de Lezama Lima*. Havana: UNEAC, 1966.

Arias, Salvador. "Nuestro primer gran poema. (Estudio de 'En el Teocalli de Cholula' de José María Heredia)." In *Nuevos críticos cubanos*, 51–104. Havana: Editorial Letras Cubanas, 1983.

Aristotle. *On the Art of Poetry*. Translated by T. S. Dorsch. New York: Penguin Books, 1965.

Arrom, José Juan. "Lo tradicional cubano en el mundo novelístico de José Lezama Lima." *Revista Iberoamericana* 41, nos. 92–93 (July-December 1975):469–77.

Ballón, José Carlos. "Autonomía cultural: de Emerson a Martí." Ph.D. diss., Stanford University, 1981.

Barradas, Efraín. "A José Lezama Lima." *Sin Nombre* 7, no. 4 (January-March 1977):44–46.

———. "José Lezama Lima: *Oppiano Licario*." *Cuadernos Hispanoamericanos* 357 (March 1980):726–28.

———. "La revista *Orígenes* (1944–1956)." Ph.D. diss., Princeton University, 1978.

Bejel, Emilio. "Cultura y Filosofía de la Historia (Spengler, Carpentier, Lezama Lima)." *Cuadernos Americanos* 239, no. 6 (November-December 1981):75–89.

———. "Cultura, Historia y Ficción en Lezama Lima." In *Annual Conference on Latin American Literature* (Montclair College). College Park: Ediciones Hispamérica, 1982.

———. "El sujeto metafórico en Lezama Lima, Valéry y Sor Juana." In *Literatura de Nuestra América*, 25–40. Xalapa: Centro de Investigaciones Lingüístico-Literarias, Universidad Veracruzana, 1983.

———. "Entrevista con Cintio Vitier." *Areíto* 27 (1981):30–34.

———. "Imagen y posibilidad en Lezama Lima." In *Coloquio internacional* ..., 1:133–42. (See *Coloquio internacional* for full reference.)

———. "Lezama o las equiprobabilidades del olvido." In *José Lezama Lima, textos críticos*, edited by Justo Ulloa, 22–37. Miami: Ediciones Universal, 1979.

———. "L'histoire et l'image de l'Amérique Latine selon Lezama Lima." *Oracl* (Poitiers) 2 (1982):92–95.

———. "'Muerte de Narciso': hacia la indiferenciación o el Paraíso." In *Literatura de Nuestra América*, 43–53. Xalapa: Centro de Investigaciones Lingüístico-Literarias, Universidad Veracruzana, 1983.

Bejel, Emilio, and Ramiro Fernández. *La subversión de la semiótica. Análisis estructural de textos hispánicos.* Gaithersburg, MD: Ediciones Hispamérica, 1988.

Bello, Andrés. "Alocución a la Poesía." In *Obras completas*, 1:43–64. Caracas: Ediciones del Ministerio de Educación, 1952.

Berlin, Isaiah. *Vico and Herder.* New York: Viking Press, 1976.

Bianchi Ross, Ciro. "Introducción." Prologue to *Imagen y posibilidad*, by José Lezama Lima, 5–17. Havana: Editorial Letras Cubanas, 1981.

Boswell, John. *Christianity, Social Tolerance, and Homosexuality.* Chicago/London: University of Chicago Press, 1980.

Cabrera Infante, Guillermo. "Encuentros y recuerdos con José Lezama Lima." *Vuelta* 3 (February 1977):47.

Carpentier, Alejo. *Concierto barroco*, 10th ed. Mexico: Siglo XXI, 1980.

———. "El papel social del novelista." In *Tientos y diferencias*, 101–19. Buenos Aires: Calicanto Editorial, 1976.

———. "La ciudad de las columnas." In *Tientos y diferencias*, 58–59.

———. "Lo barroco y lo real maravilloso." In *Razón de ser*, 61–64. Caracas: Universidad Central de Venezuela, Ediciones del Rectorado, 1976.

Casal, Lourdes. *El caso Padilla.* Miami: Ediciones Universal, 1971.

Coleridge, Samuel Taylor. *Biographia Literaria.* New York: Macmillan, 1926.

Collingwood, R. G. "Oswald Spengler and the Theory of Historical Cycles." *Antiquity* 1 (1927):311–25, 435–46.

Coloquio internacional sobre la obra de José Lezama Lima, edited by Cristina Vizcaíno and Eugenio Suárez Galván. (Centre de Recherches Latinamericaines Université de Poitiers). 2 vols. Madrid: Editorial Fundamentos, 1984.

Cortázar, Julio. "An Approach to Lezama Lima." *Review* 12 (Fall 1974):20–25.

———. "José Lezama Lima, 1910–1976: An Ever-Present Beacon." *Review* 18 (Fall 1976):30.

———. "Literatura en la revolución y revolución en la literatura." *Marcha* (9 January 1970):30–31.

Cruz, Arnaldo. "*Paradiso* de José Lezama Lima: una problemática de los orígenes." Ph.D. diss., Stanford University, 1984.

Curtius, Ernest. *Marcel Proust y Paul Valéry.* Translated by Pedro Lecuona. Buenos Aires: Losada, 1941.

de la Cruz, Sor Juana Inés. *El divino Narciso.* In *Obras selectas.* Prologue, selection, and notes by Georgina Sabat de Rivers and Elias L. Rivers, pp. 128–91. Barcelona: Editorial Noguer, 1978.

Echevarren, Roberto. "Lezama Lima y Severo Sarduy: una poética del neobarroco." *La Gaceta del Fondo de Cultura Económica* 7, no. 75 (March 1977):10–12.

Ferguson, Frances C. "Reading Heidegger: Paul DeMan and Jacques Derrida." In *Martin Heidegger and the Question of Literature,* edited by William V. Spanos, 253–70. Bloomington/London: Indiana University Press, 1976.

Fernández Retamar, Roberto. *La poesía contemporánea en Cuba (1927–53).* Havana: Orígenes, 1954.

———. "La poesía de José Lezama Lima." In *Recopilación de textos sobre José Lezama Lima,* edited by Pedro Simón Martínez, 90–99. Havana: Casa de las Américas, Serie valoración múltiple, 1970.

Fernández-Sosa, Luis Francisco. *José Lezama Lima y la crítica anagógica.* Miami: Ediciones Universal, 1977.

Franco, Jean. "Lezama Lima en el paraíso de la poesía." *Vórtice* 1, no. 1 (Spring 1974):30–48.

García Marruz, Fina. "Por *Dador* de José Lezama Lima." In *Recopilación de textos sobre José Lezama Lima,* edited by Pedro Simón Martínez, 107–26. Havana: Casa de las Américas, Serie valoración múltiple, 1970.

García Marruz, Graciela. "La obra poética de Cintio Vitier." Ph.D. diss., City University of New York, 1982.

Genette, Gérard. "Complejo de Narciso." Translated by Nora Rosenfeld and María Cristina Mata, in *Figuras,* 23–31. Córdoba, Argentina: Ediciones Nagelkop, 1970.

———. "Valéry and the Poetics of Language." In *Textual Strategies,* edited by Josué V. Harari, 359–73. Ithaca: Cornell University Press, 1979.

Gimbernat de González, Ester. *Paradiso: entre los confines de la transgresión.* Xalapa: Universidad Veracruzana, 1982.

González, Reynaldo. "Entre la magia y la infinitud." In *Lezama Lima: el ingenuo culpable,* pp. 140–42. Havana: Letras Cubanas, 1988.

González Echevarría, Roberto. *Alejo Carpentier: The Pilgrim at Home.* Ithaca: Cornell University Press, 1977.

———. "Apetitos de Góngora y Lezama." In *Relecturas: estudios de literatura cubana,* 95–118. Caracas: Monte Ávila Editores, 1976.

———. "Lo cubano en *Paradiso.*" In *Coloquio internacional . . . ,* 2: 31–51. (See *Coloquio internacional* for full reference.)

Goytisolo, José Agustín, ed. *Posible imagen de José Lezama Lima.* Barcelona: Libres de Sinera, 1969.

Grases, Pedro. Prologue to Andrés Bello, *Antología de Andrés Bello.* Caracas: Kapelusz, 1954.

Hart Dávalos, Armando. "Entrevista." *El País* (March 14, 1983), also published in *Cambiar las reglas del juego.* Havana: Editorial Letras Cubanas, 1983.

Heidegger, Martin. "Nietzsche as Metaphysician." Translated by Joan Stambaugh, in *Nietzsche. A Collection of Critical Essays*, edited by Robert C. Solomon, pp. 105-13. Garden City, NY: Anchor Press/Doubleday, 1973.

Heredia, José María. "Renunciando a la poesía." In *Poesías*. New York: Librería de Behr y Kahl, 1825.

Hill, John Spencer, ed. *Imagination in Coleridge*. Totowa, NJ: Rowman and Littlefield, 1978.

Hollingsworth, Charles. "The Development of Literary Theory in Cuba, 1959-1968." Ph.D. diss., University of California, Berkeley, 1972.

Holub, Renate Wiesner. "Problematics of Giambattista Vico's Theory of Poetics and Aesthetics." Ph.D. diss., University of Wisconsin, 1983.

Hoy, David Couzens. "The Owl and the Poet: Heidegger's Critique of Hegel." In *Martin Heidegger and the Question of Literature*, edited by William V. Spanos, 53-70. Bloomington/London: Indiana University Press, 1976.

Jay, Paul. *Being in the Text*. Ithaca/London: Cornell University Press, 1984.

Jitrik, Noé. "Paradiso entre desborde y ruptura." *Texto crítico* 5, no. 13 (April-June 1979):71-89.

Junco Fazzolari, Margarita. *Paradiso y el sistema poético de Lezama Lima*. Buenos Aires: Fernando García Gambeiro, 1979.

Koch, Dolores M. "Dos poemas de Lezama Lima: el primero y el postrero." *Coloquio Internacional . . .*, 1:143-55. (See *Coloquio internacional* for full reference.)

Lacan, Jacques. *Écrits*. Paris: Seuil, 1966.

Lezama Lima, Eloísa. "Mi hermano." In *José Lezama Lima, textos críticos*, edited by Justo Ulloa, 11-17. Miami: Ediciones Universal, 1979.

———. "Para leer *Paradiso*." In her edition of *Paradiso*, 13-17.

———. "*Paradiso*: una novela poema." In her edition of *Paradiso*, 47-94.

———. "Un sistema poético del universo." In her edition of *Paradiso*, 31-46.

———. "Vida, pasión y creación de José Lezama Lima: fechas claves para una cronología." In her edition of *Paradiso*, 16-40.

Lihn, Enrique. "*Paradiso*: novela y homosexualidad." *Hispamérica* 22 (1979):3-21.

Lope, Monique de. "Narcise Ailé. Etude sur 'Muerte de Narciso' (1937) de José Lezama Lima." *Caravelle. Cahiers du Monde Hispanique et Luso-Brésilien* 29 (1977):25-44.

Mañach, Jorge. "El arcano de cierta poesía nueva. Carta abierta al poeta José Lezama Lima." *Bohemia* 39 (25 September 1949):78, 90.

———. "Reacciones a un diálogo literario (Algo más sobre poesía vieja y nueva)." *Bohemia* 42 (16 October 1949):63, 107.

Martí, José. "Emerson." In *Obras completas*, 17–30. Havana: Editorial de Ciencias Sociales, 1975.

Martínez, José Luis. "La obra de Alfonso Reyes." *Cuadernos Americanos* (January-February 1952):109–29.

Mazzotta, Giuseppe. *Dante, Poet of the Desert*. Princeton: Princeton University Press, 1979.

Mignolo, Walter. "*Paradiso*: desviación y red." *Texto crítico* 5, no. 13 (April-June 1979):90–101.

Moran, John, editor and translator. *Rousseau—Herder: On the Origin of Language*. New York: F. Ungar, 1967.

Moraña, Mabel. "Literatura y cultura nacional en Hispanoamérica (*1910-1940*)." Ph.D. diss., University of Minnesota, 1983.

Moreno Fraginals, Manuel. "Lezama Lima y la Revolución." *Plural* 6, no. 74 (November 1977):14–18.

———. "Prólogo." In *Oppiano Licario*, by José Lezama Lima. Havana: Editorial Arte y Literatura, 1977.

Moscoso-Góngora, Peter. "A Proust of the Caribbean." *The Nation* (USA) (11 May 1974):600–601.

O'Gorman, Edmundo. "Teoría del deslinde y deslinde de la Teoría." *Filosofía y Letras* 17 (January–March 1945):21–36.

Ortega, Julio. "La biblioteca de José Cemí." *Revista Iberoamericana* 41, nos. 92–93 (July-December 1975):509–21.

———. "*La expresión americana*: una teoría de la cultura." *Eco* 187 (May 1977):55–63.

———. "Language as Hero." *Review* 12 (Fall 1974):35–42.

———. "Lezama Lima." In *Relato de utopía: Notas sobre narrativa cubana de la revolución*, 51–97. Barcelona: La Gaya Ciencia, 1973.

———. "Paradiso." In *La contemplación y la fiesta: ensayos sobre la novela hispanoamericana*, 2d ed., 77–116. Caracas: Monte Ávila, 1969.

———. "Reading *Paradiso*." In *Poetics of Change*, 60–84. Austin: University of Texas Press, 1984.

Ortega, Julio, and Ester Gimbernat de González. "Prólogo." In *El reino de la imagen*. Caracas: Biblioteca Ayacucho, 1981.

Otero, Lisandro. "Para una definición mejor de Lezama Lima." *Boletín del Círculo de Cultura Cubana* (August 1983).

Padilla, Heberto. "La poesía en su lugar." *Lunes de Revolución* 38 (7 December 1959):5–6.

———. "Lezama Lima frente a su discurso." *Linden Lane Magazine* 1, no. 1 (January-March 1982):16–18.

Palmer, Richard E. "The Postmodernity of Heidegger." In *Martin Heidegger and the Question of Literature*, edited by William V. Spanos, 71–92. Bloomington/London: Indiana University Press, 1976.

Paz, Octavio. *Los hijos del limo*. Barcelona: Seix-Barral, 1974.

Pellón, Gustavo. *"Paradiso:* un fibroma de diecisiete libras." *Hispamérica 9*, nos. 25–26 (1980):147–51.

———. "Portrait of the Cuban Writer as French Painter: Henri Rousseau, José Lezama Lima's Alter Ego." *Modern Language Notes* 103, no. 2 (March 1988):350–73.

Pereira, Manuel. "José Lezama Lima: las cartas sobre la mesa." In *Coloquio internacional* ... , 1:103–22. (See *Coloquio internacional* for full reference.)

Pérez Firmat, Gustavo. "Descent into *Paradiso:* A Study of Heaven and Homosexuality." *Hispania* 59 (1976):247–57.

Pézard, André. "La langue italienne dans la pensée de Dante." *Cahiers du Sud* 34 (1951):25–38.

Philostratus. *Imagines*. Translated by Arthur Fairbanks. London/New York: Loeb Classical Library, 1931.

Piedra, Armando J. "La revista cubana *Orígenes* (1944–56): portavoz generacional." Ph.D. diss., University of Florida, 1977.

Portuondo, José Antonio. *Bosquejo histórico de las letras cubanas*. Havana: Ministerio de Relaciones Exteriores, 1960.

Poulet, Georges. *The Interior Distance*. Translated by Elliott Coleman. Ann Arbor: University of Michigan Press, 1964.

Prats Sariol, José. "Poesía póstuma de José Lezama Lima." *Casa de las Américas* 19, no. 112 (January-February 1979):143–49.

———. "La revista *Orígenes*." In *Coloquio internacional* ... , 1:37–57. (See *Coloquio internacional* for full reference.)

Praz, Mario. *Studies in Seventeenth-Century Imagery*. 2d ed. Rome: Sussidi eruditi, 1964.

Riccio, Alessandra. "Los años de *Orígenes*." In *Coloquio internacional* ... , 1:21–36. (See *Coloquio internacional* for full reference.)

Richard, J. P. *L'univers imaginaire de Mallarmé*. Paris: Seuil, 1961.

Riddle, Joseph N. "From Heidegger to Derrida to Chance: Doubling and (Poetic) Language." In *Martin Heidegger and the Question of Literature*, edited by William V. Spanos, 231–52. Bloomington/London: Indiana University Press, 1976.

Ríos-Ávila, Rubén. "A Theology of Absence: The Poetic System of José Lezama Lima." Ph.D. diss., Cornell University, 1983.

———. "L'image comme système." *Oracl* (Poitiers) 2 (1982):96–100.

———. "The Origin and the Island: Lezama and Mallarmé." *Latin American Literary Review* 8, no. 16 (Spring-Summer 1980):242–55.

Rivera-Rodas, Oscar. "Teoría hispanoamericana de la poesía: 1823–1920." Ph.D. diss., University of California, Davis, 1980.

Rodríguez Monegal, Emir. *"Paradiso* en su contexto." *Mundo Nuevo* 24 (June 1968):40–44.

———. *"Paradiso:* Una silogística del sobresalto." *Revista Iberoamericana* 41, nos. 92–93 (July-December 1975):523–33.

Santí, Enrico Mario. "Hacia Oppiano Licario." *Revista Iberoamericana* 47, nos. 116–17 (July-December 1981):273–79.

———. "La invención de Lezama Lima." *Vuelta* 102 (May 1985):45–52.

———. "*Oppiano Licario*, la poética del fragmento." In *Coloquio internacional ...* , 2:135–51. (See *Coloquio internacional* for full references.)

———. "Parridiso." *Modern Language Notes* 94 (1979):343–65.

Sarduy, Severo. *Barroco*. Buenos Aires: Editorial Sudamericana, 1977.

———. "A Cuban Proust." *Review* 12 (Fall 1974):43–45.

———. "Carta de Lezama." *Voces* 2 (1982):33–41.

———. "Dispersión/Falsas notas: homenaje a Lezama." In *Escrito sobre un cuerpo*, 61–89. Buenos Aires: Editorial Sudamericana, 1969.

———. "Oppiano Licario: el libro que no podía concluir." *Punto de Contacto / Point of Contact* 2, nos. 3–4 (Winter 1981):123–31.

Schulman, Ivan. *Símbolo y color en la obra de José Martí*. Madrid: Gredos, 1970.

Shelley, Percy B. *A Defense of Poetry*. In *Complete Works*, edited by Roger Ingspen and Walter E. Peck, 107–40. New York: Gordian Press, 1965.

Souza, Raymond. *The Poetic Fiction of José Lezama Lima*. Columbia: University of Missouri Press, 1983.

Spengler, Oswald. *The Decline of the West*. Translated by Charles Francis Atkinson. 2 vols. New York: Alfred A. Knopf, 1928.

Suárez-Galván, Eugenio. "Una obra ignorada: los cuentos de Lezama." In *Coloquio internacional ...* , 2:7–18. (See *Coloquio internacional* for full reference.)

Uitti, Karl D. *Linguistics and Literary Theory*. Englewood Cliffs, NJ: Prentice-Hall, 1969.

Ulloa, Leonor Álvarez de. "El proceso creativo del ensayismo de José Lezama Lima." Ph.D. diss., University of Kentucky, 1979.

———. "Ordenamiento secreto de la poética de Lezama." In *José Lezama Lima, textos críticos*, edited by Justo Ulloa, 38–65. Miami: Ediciones Universal, 1979.

Ulloa, Justo. "La narrativa de Lezama Lima y Sarduy: entre la imagen visionaria y el juego verbal." Ph.D. diss., University of Kentucky, 1973.

———. *Sobre José Lezama Lima y sus lectores: guía y compendio bibliográfico*. Boulder: Society of Spanish and Spanish-American Studies, 1987.

Valéry, Paul. "Fragments du Narcise." Translated by Cintio Vitier in *Orígenes* 2, no. 23 (1949):11–16.

———. *Œuvres*, volume 1. Paris: Pléiade, 1957.

Van den Berg, J.H. "The Subject and His Landscape." In *Romanticism and Consciousness*, edited by Harold Bloom, pp. 57–65. New York: Norton, 1979.

Vargas Llosa, Mario. "Attempting the impossible." *Review* 12 (Fall 1974):26–29.

Verene, Donald Phillip. *Vico's Science of Imagination.* Ithaca: Cornell University Press, 1981.

Vico, Giambattista. *The New Science.* Translated from the 1944 3d ed. by Thomas Goddard Bergin and Max Harold Fisch. Ithaca: Cornell University Press, 1948.

Villa, Álvaro de, and José Sánchez Boudy. *Lezama Lima: peregrino inmóvil (Paradiso al desnudo).* Miami: Ediciones Universal, 1974.

Vinge, Louise. *The Narcissus Theme in Western European Literature up to the Early Nineteenth Century.* Translated from Swedish by Robert Dewnap in collaboration with Lisbeth Grönlind, Nigel Reeves, and Ingrid Söderberg Reeves. Lind: Skdnska Centraltrycheriet, 1967.

Vitier, Cintio. "De las cartas que me escribió Lezama." In *Coloquio internacional . . . ,* 1:277–92. (See *Coloquio internacional* for full reference.)

———. " Introducción a la obra de José Lezama Lima." In José Lezama Lima, *Obras completas,* vol. 1. Mexico: Aguilar, 1975.

———. "La poesía de José Lezama Lima y el intento de una teleología insular." In *Recopilación de textos sobre José Lezama Lima,* edited by Pedro Simón Martínez, pp. 68–89. Havana: Casa de las Américas, 1970.

———. "Martí y Darío en Lezama." *Cuadernos Americanos* 26, no. 152 (September-October 1985):4–13.

Vitier, Cintio, and Fina García Marruz. "Respuesta a Armando Álvarez Bravo." In *Coloquio internacional . . . ,* 1:99–102.

Worringer, Wilhelm. *Form in Gothic.* Translated by Herbert Read. New York: Schocken Books, 1957.

Zambrano, María. "La Cuba secreta." *Orígenes* 5, no. 20 (1948):3–9.

Index

Abatón (character in *Oppiano Licario*), 121
About Cuban Restlessness (Marinello's *Sobre la inquietud cubana*), 137
Abrams, Meyer, 24
Absence of natural order, 16, 72–73, 81–83, 95–96, 111
Acrisio, myth of, 60
Adam, myth of, 46, 141
African culture, 135, 136, 141
Afro-Cuban religion, 99
"Ah, that you flee!" (Lezama's poem "¡Ah, que tú escapes!"), 29
Alberto (character in *Paradiso*), 80, 83, 100, 114
Aleijandinho, 134, 135, 142
Aleixandre, Vicente: represented in *Orígenes*, 11
Aletheia, Heidegger's concept of, 52–53
Alienation, 10, 72
American and Cuban Literary Expression (Marinello's *Americanismos y cubanismos literarios*), 137
American being, idea of, 146–47
American Expression, The (Lezama's essay collection *La expresión americana*), 119–20, 128, 140–41
Americanism, 9, 136, 137, 138, 140
Americanists, 9, 136
Amerindian world, 138, 140

Amo (character in Carpentier's *Baroque Concert*), 142–43
Andrés (character in *Paradiso*), 80
Apollo, myth of, 51.
APRA (Alianza Popular Revolucionaria Americana; Popular Revolutionary American Alliance—Peruvian political organization), 136
Aquinas, Thomas, 86
Aragon, Louis: represented in *Orígenes*, 11
Aristotle, 21
"Ateneo de la Juventud" (Athenaeum of Youth—Mexican cultural group), 136, 137
Atlantis, myth of, 137
Atrio Flaminio (character in *Paradiso*), 98
Augusta (character in *Paradiso*), 78–79, 98
Augustine, Saint, 6, 52, 86; *Confessions*, 28, 76–78, 103
Autobiographical narrative, 75–78, 103–5
Avance, Revista de (Cuban avant-garde magazine), 17–18, 137, 138
Avant-garde style, 17–21
Ayala, Francisco: represented in *Orígenes*, 11
Azar concurrente (synchronicity of fate), Lezama's concept of, 99
Aztec mythology, 135

Bach, Johann Sebastian, 114, 125
Bacon, Roger, 50–51,

About the Author

Emilio Bejel received his Ph.D. in Spanish from Florida State University (Tallahassee) in 1970, and at the present time is Professor of Spanish American literature at the University of Florida (Gainesville). He also taught at Fairfield University from 1971 to 1982. Professor Bejel has given special seminars on Spanish American literature and literary theory at the universities of Yale, Union, Rosario (Argentina), and Pedro Henríquez Ureña (Dominican Republic).

As a critic, Bejel has written numerous articles and four previous books: *Buero Vallejo: lo moral, lo social y lo metafísico* (1972), *Literatura de Nuestra América* (1984), *La subversión de la semiótica. Análisis estructural de textos hispánicos* (co-authored with Professor Ramiro Fernández) (1988), and *Escribir en Cuba. Imagen de los 80* (in press).

His poetry collections include *Del aire y la piedra* (1974), *Ese viaje único* (1977), *Direcciones y Paraísos* (1977), *Huellas/Footprints* (with English recreations by Professor Marie Panico) (1982), and *Casas deshabitadas* (with illustrations by Vicente Dopico) (1989).

About the Illustrator

The illustrator of this volume, Vicente Dopico, was born in Havana, Cuba, in 1943. He has lived in the United States since the early sixties. In 1974, he received his Bachelor of Arts degree from the University of St. Thomas in Miami. In 1976, from the same university, he obtained his Master of Science in social sciences and education. Also in 1976 he won the Cintas Foundation Prize in painting and drawing. Florida Atlantic University honored him with its First Prize in Painting during the academic year 1970–71.

His paintings and drawings have been exhibited in the Miami Art Center, Miami Dade Community College, Florida Atlantic University, Winter Park Museum of Art, Museum of Fine Arts, Art Student League (New York), Spanish Fair (New York), San Bernardino Museum of Art (California), and La Galería (Santo Domingo, Dominican Republic).

Mr. Dopico's most accomplished works are drawings and watercolors. His works are held in collections in Spain, France, and Spanish America as well as the United States. His art has been influenced by such Cuban painters as René Portocarrero and José María Mijares, and he acknowledges the influence on his style of the works of Willem de Kooning and Francis Bacon.

Library of Congress Cataloging-in-Publication Data

Bejel, Emilio, 1944–
    José Lezama Lima, poet of the image / Emilio Bejel.
        p.   cm.   —   (University of Florida monographs. Humanities no.64)
        Includes bibliographical references.
        ISBN 0-8130-0980-4 (alk. paper)
        1. Lezama Lima, José—Criticism and interpretation. I. Title.
    II. Series.
    PQ7389.L49Z58   1990   89–20389
    861—dc20   CIP